PENGUIN BO(

Slow Food

BIBLE

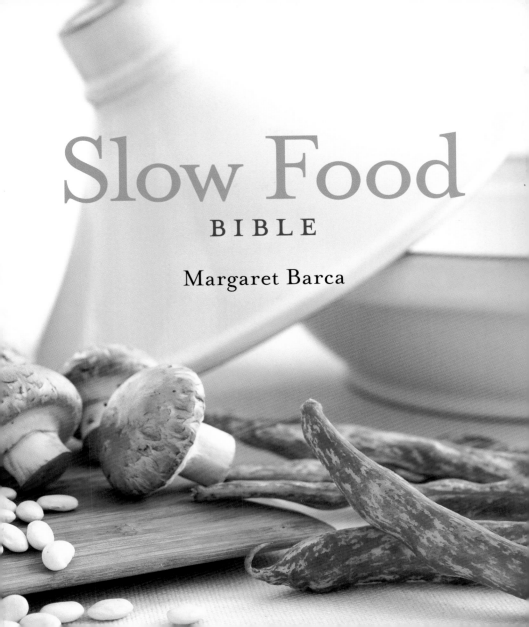

Slow Food

BIBLE

Margaret Barca

Contents

Introduction   1

Slow food basics   3

Soups   13

Seafood   41

Chicken, duck & rabbit   55

Beef, lamb, pork & veal   91

Vegetables & sides   189

Sweets   223

Conversions   250

Index   251

Introduction

Slow food does not mean taking forever to roast or braise a piece of meat. It is about taking time to enjoy food — the choosing, the cooking, the delight in sharing good food with family and friends. It's about fresh and seasonal ingredients, as natural and as wholesome as possible.

And slow certainly doesn't have to mean complicated or hard to cook or prepare. Many of the recipes in this book are quite simple, and for most of the time you can get on with other things or — better still — just kick back, relax and enjoy the aromas while the dish simmers away on top of the stove or in the oven.

Slow food basics

For most cultures, slow cooking is an age-old tradition, designed to extract maximum flavour and goodness from basic ingredients.

Braise, casserole or stew — what's the difference? Usually (but not always), for a braise, meat is most often browned on top of the stove to give it colour and depth of flavour, and then combined with other ingredients and a small amount of liquid, covered and cooked gently for a long time, on top of the stove or in the oven. For a stew or casserole, more liquid is used and the cooking time is often shorter.

One of the advantages of dishes slow-baked in the oven is that there is far less chance of your meat or vegetables sticking to the bottom of the pot. When braising or stewing on the stove-top, adjust the heat to the lowest setting and keep the lid on the pot (unless the recipe specifies otherwise) to keep steam and moisture trapped within. A heavy-based saucepan — for example, of enamelled cast iron — is ideal for slow cooking, but a stove-top heat diffuser will help compensate for saucepans that are not so heavy.

Slow-cooking meat

Long, slow cooking is the perfect way to tenderise meat and allow rich, full-bodied flavours to develop. It is also an economical way to cook — many of the meats most suited to slow cooking are less expensive cuts. And minimising waste by using cuts of meat that in some societies have been deemed too humble, such as shanks and tail, is a way of showing respect for both the animal and the environment.

SOME CUTS SUITABLE FOR BRAISES AND STEWS

beef
Chuck steak, blade (or oyster blade) steak, round steak, topside, fresh silverside, skirt steak, gravy beef, shank, ox tail.

chicken and duck

Chicken on the bone (such as maryland, legs, thighs and wings) is best for slow cooking — it definitely has more flavour. The same goes for duck, which is also available in jointed pieces, from markets and specialist butchers.

lamb

Shoulder, leg or forequarter (boned, or bone left in), shanks, neck.

rabbit

Both farmed and wild rabbits are now fairly widely available — wild rabbits have a slightly more gamey flavour. Usually rabbits are sold whole, but you can ask your butcher to cut it into portions.

pork

Shoulder, forequarter chops, rump.

veal

Brisket, shanks, neck, shoulder, silverside, topside.

TIPS FOR SLOW-COOKING MEAT

- When browning meat, don't put too much in at one time, as it will take longer to brown and may start to stew rather than get a nice 'toasted' finish.

- Long, slow cooking releases natural fats from meat, so later in the cooking process you may need to skim excess fat from the surface of a braise or stew. If the dish is refrigerated overnight, the fat will settle and set on the surface and you can remove it more easily before reheating the dish.

- Unless a recipe states otherwise, always stew and braise with a snugly fitting lid on the dish, to retain moisture. You can also place aluminium foil or buttered, non-stick baking paper directly on top of the ingredients or under the lid to help reduce evaporation.

- Leave slow-roasted (or any roasted) meats to stand for 10–15 minutes before slicing and serving. The meat will be easier to carve and more tender to eat.

- Most slow-cooked dishes improve when left overnight or for several days, which allows the flavours to develop, mingle and intensify.

Slow-cooking pulses

Pulses (dried beans, peas and lentils) are intrinsic to slow cooking in many cultures — lentils are used to make Indian dhal, beans are the base for hearty soups and stews in many parts of Europe, and chickpeas also star in many cuisines.

Soak pulses in plenty of fresh water (twice the volume of water to beans is ideal). If you can't, or forget to, soak them overnight, put them in a saucepan, bring to the boil and simmer for 10 minutes, then turn off heat and leave to soak for an hour or so before cooking.

Once cooked and drained, pulses can be kept refrigerated for two to three days.

CAN YOU USE A CAN?

For some recipes, if you are short of time you can use canned pulses, but be aware that canned beans and lentils tend to lose their shape and so are best used only in an emergency (add them at the end of the cooking time). Chickpeas retain more of their texture and flavour, but should still be added at the end of cooking.

Using a crockpot or slow-cooker

The recipes in this book suit both stove-top and oven cooking, but crockpots (often now simply called slow-cookers) are an excellent solution, especially if it suits you to have a dish simmering away while you are at work or away from home for a few hours. These cookers operate on an extremely low temperature, with the heat very evenly distributed.

Check the instructions for your particular model, as most have conversion times for standard recipes. You could leave a stew to cook gently for 8–10 hours on the lowest setting, or you can hurry it along by setting the cooker to High and braising for only 4–5 hours.

TIPS FOR USING SLOW-COOKERS

- If you are adapting a conventional recipe, you will often need slightly less liquid, as slow-cookers are very well sealed and retain the cooking juices and moisture.

- Every time you lift the lid, steam and moisture escape and increase the cooking time, so it's best not to look too often. One good way to avoid this lid-lifting is to choose a slow-cooker or crockpot with a glass lid.

- If a recipe calls for milk, cream, yoghurt or cheese, it is best to add these near the end of cooking, in the last hour or so, as dairy products can separate during the slow cooking.

Soups

Soup is comfort food and possibly the ultimate slow food: a heart-warming and usually hearty bowl of goodness that may be rich with vegetables, dense with slow-simmered meat or studded with pulses, or fragrant with herbs.

It seems the tradition of soup is as old as the history of food itself, with the word itself derived from the classical Latin suppa. In the Middle Ages it was a restorative dish consisting of bread soaked in nutritious liquid and it is still customary to serve bread with soup. The classic French onion soup maintains the tradition of the bread in the liquid, its cheesy toasts soaked in a dense onion-rich broth.

The best soup begins with a flavoursome stock. Take the time to make one and you will be surprised at the additional depth of flavour in your soups.

‹ Beef stock (page 14)

Beef stock

500 g beef shin, diced

500 g beef marrow bones,
  cut into quarters

1 onion, halved

2 carrots, peeled and
  roughly chopped

4 stalks celery, roughly chopped

1 bay leaf

2 sprigs fresh parsley

1 sprig fresh thyme

4 black peppercorns

salt

3 litres water

Place all ingredients in a large stockpot. Bring to the boil, remove any scum from the surface, then reduce heat, partially cover and simmer very gently for 2 hours. Check and skim surface occasionally.

Strain stock, and refrigerate when cool. When cold, remove any fat from the surface. The stock will keep for 2–3 days in the refrigerator, or can be frozen.

 For a darker, richer beef stock, place everything except the water in a roasting pan and roast in a hot oven for 45 minutes until meat and vegetables are coloured. Then transfer to stockpot, add water and proceed as above.

MAKES 2 LITRES

Chicken stock

1.5 kg chicken (whole or pieces)

3.5 litres water

1 onion, sliced

1 carrot, peeled and chopped

1 leek, white part only, sliced

1 stalk celery, sliced

1 bay leaf

1 sprig fresh thyme

2 sprigs fresh parsley

6 black peppercorns

Rinse the chicken well, place in a large stockpot and add 3.5 litres of water (the chicken should be completely covered). Bring to simmering point, then skim the surface. Add the vegetables and herbs, and bring just to the boil. Reduce heat to low and simmer very gently for 1½–2 hours. Don't let it boil or the stock will be cloudy.

Allow stock to cool a little, then strain. Discard the vegetables and herbs (keep the meat for sandwiches). Refrigerate stock and remove fat from the surface once it has set.

If you want a stronger stock, return stock to heat and boil to reduce. The stock keeps in the refrigerator for 3–4 days, or can be frozen.

MAKES ABOUT 3 LITRES

Chicken noodle soup

2 kg chicken (whole or pieces)

1 brown onion, quartered

2 large carrots, peeled and
then halved lengthwise

5 stalks celery, chopped

1 bay leaf

2 sprigs fresh parsley

2.5 litres water

1 teaspoon salt

freshly ground black pepper

180 g vermicelli noodles

3 tablespoons chopped
flat-leaf parsley

Place the chicken, vegetables, bay leaf and parsley sprigs in a large pot and cover with the water. Bring slowly to the boil, removing any scum from the surface.

Lower heat, and season with the salt and pepper. Cover and simmer gently (do not let it boil) for 2 hours, or until meat is falling off the bones.

Now remove the chicken from the broth, pull meat from the bones and shred it. Return the carcass and bones to the broth and simmer for a further hour.

Pour the cooking liquid through a fine strainer into a bowl, leave to cool and then refrigerate overnight. The liquid will solidify into jelly with a layer of fat on top. Carefully remove the fat. **>**

To serve, gently reheat the broth, add the noodles and shredded chicken, and simmer for 5–6 minutes. Stir in the chopped parsley, and check seasoning before serving.

SERVES 6

Chickpea & pancetta soup

400 g dried chickpeas

100 g butter

150 g pancetta, chopped

2 onions, finely chopped

1 medium-sized carrot, peeled and finely chopped

½ teaspoon ground sweet paprika

1 bay leaf

2 cloves garlic, cut in half

salt and freshly ground black pepper

fresh coriander leaves, and extra ground sweet paprika, to serve

Cover the chickpeas with water and soak overnight. Drain, place in a saucepan with plenty of cold water, bring to the boil and simmer for 20 minutes. Drain and set aside.

Melt the butter in a large saucepan over medium heat. Add the pancetta and sauté until starting to turn golden-brown. Add the onions, carrot and sweet paprika. Sauté for 5–6 minutes, stirring occasionally, until vegetables are softened.

Add the drained chickpeas, bay leaf, garlic and enough water to cover. Bring to the boil, partially cover with a lid, lower the heat and simmer for 45–60 minutes. ➤

Leave the soup to cool a little, then process in batches in a blender until smooth. Season with salt and freshly ground pepper, and return to a clean saucepan to reheat gently.

To serve, ladle into bowls and scatter with some coriander leaves and a light dusting of ground sweet paprika.

SERVES 4–6

Classic pea & ham soup

2 tablespoons vegetable oil

2 onions, thinly sliced

1 ham hock (about 1.2 kg)
 — ask your butcher to cut it into 3 pieces

3 litres cold water

500 g split green peas

salt and freshly ground black pepper

croutons, to serve

Heat oil in a large, heavy-based saucepan over low heat. Add onion and sauté for 10–15 minutes, stirring occasionally, until caramelised. Add ham hock and cold water. Bring to the boil, skim the surface, partially cover, then simmer for 1½ hours.

Remove the hock, cut away any skin, slice off the meat and chop coarsely. Cover and set aside.

Rinse peas then add to soup, cover and simmer for 2 hours until peas break down and soup is thick. Season with salt and freshly ground pepper. Add meat to soup and heat through.

To serve, ladle into bowls and sprinkle with a few croutons.

SERVES 6

French onion soup

100 g unsalted butter

2 kg onions, thinly sliced

salt and freshly ground black pepper

½ cup dry white wine

4 cups beef stock (page 14)

fresh bouquet garni (see note page 25)

8 slices French breadstick, 2 cm thick

200 g grated gruyere cheese

Melt the butter in a large, heavy-based saucepan. Add onions, season with salt and pepper, then cover and cook, stirring occasionally, for 15 minutes. The onions should be soft and starting to colour. Add wine, increase heat and cook for 3–4 minutes until liquid has almost evaporated. Add 1 cup of stock, reduce heat and cook gently for 1 hour, stirring occasionally. The onions should be caramelised.

Add remaining stock and bouquet garni, bring to the boil, reduce heat and simmer, partially covered, for about 30 minutes. The soup should be quite thick. Test for seasoning and remove bouquet garni.

Preheat oven to 180°C. ➤

Lightly toast bread slices. Place four ovenproof bowls on an oven tray, and ladle soup into each bowl. Sprinkle a little cheese over the soup, then top with toast slices and sprinkle with more cheese. Place in preheated oven for about 5 minutes. When cheese is melted and bubbling, the soup is ready to serve.

 To make a fresh bouquet garni, take 3 sprigs of parsley, 1 sprig of marjoram, 1 sprig of thyme and 2 bay leaves, and tie tightly together with kitchen string (or wrap in muslin or cheesecloth and tie tightly). A piece of orange or lemon zest is a tasty addition. You can buy dried bouquets garni, but the fresh version adds a lovely subtle flavour.

SERVES 4

Harira soup

2–3 tablespoons olive oil

500 g lamb leg or shoulder, diced

2 onions, finely diced

1 red capsicum, diced

2 cloves garlic, finely chopped

2 teaspoons ground ginger

1 teaspoon ground turmeric

1 cup dried chickpeas, soaked for 8 hours, rinsed and drained

1.5 litres chicken stock (page 15) or beef stock (page 14)

1.5 kg tomatoes, peeled, seeded and coarsely chopped

1 cup small green lentils

freshly squeezed lemon juice, to taste

salt and freshly ground black pepper

ground cinnamon and chopped fresh coriander leaves, to serve

Heat the oil in a large stockpot. Cook the lamb in batches until well browned. Remove from pan and set aside.

Add a little more oil to the pan if necessary, then add the onions, capsicum and garlic and sauté until vegetables are soft.

Return lamb to the pot and add ginger, turmeric, drained chickpeas and stock. Bring to the boil and skim the surface. Add the tomatoes and simmer for about 1–1½ hours, until chickpeas and lamb are soft. **>**

Pick over the lentils to remove any grit, place lentils in a separate pot, cover with fresh water, bring to the boil, then drain and rinse well under cold water before adding to the soup. Cook for about 20 minutes, or until soft.

Before serving, stir the lemon juice through and season with salt and pepper to taste. Ladle into bowls, dust with cinnamon and sprinkle generously with fresh coriander.

 This Moroccan soup is traditionally eaten to break the fast at the end of each day during the Muslim holy month of Ramadan. The coriander adds a fresh touch, or you can add fresh mint. Serve with pita or other flat bread.

SERVES 6

La ribollita

300 g dried cannellini beans

4 tablespoons olive oil

2 cloves garlic, finely chopped

2 medium-sized onions, diced

2 stalks celery, finely sliced

1 medium-sized carrot, peeled and finely sliced

2 tablespoons finely chopped flat-leaf parsley

500 g silverbeet, washed and shredded

800 g cavolo nero (a dark-green kale), washed and shredded

1 tablespoon tomato paste

3 litres water

salt and freshly ground black pepper

8 slices ciabatta or similar bread

extra-virgin olive oil, to serve

Check the beans for any impurities, then rinse and soak in cold water overnight. Drain the beans, place in a saucepan, cover with plenty of cold water and bring to the boil. Remove any scum from the surface, lower the heat and simmer, uncovered, for about 1 hour until the beans are tender.

Drain the beans and purée about one-third of them with a little of the cooking water, then set aside both the whole and the puréed beens.

Heat oil in a heavy-based saucepan. Add garlic, onions, celery, carrot and parsley and sauté for 5 minutes until vegetables are soft. Add silverbeet and cavolo nero, and sauté until they have softened. ➤

Add tomato paste and water, and bring to the boil. Lower heat and simmer for about 1 hour. Stir in cooked beans (whole and puréed) and simmer for another 15 minutes.

Ideally, leave the soup overnight for the flavours to develop. Next day, reheat the soup and season with salt and pepper. Lightly toast or grill bread.

To serve, place toasted bread slice in the base of each bowl. Ladle soup over, and add a drizzle of extra-virgin olive oil.

 The Italian word *ribollita* literally means reboiled – the soup is made, left to 'mature' overnight, then boiled again and bread and extra olive oil added. If you can't find cavolo nero, use cabbage or fresh spinach instead.

SERVES 8

Lamb & lima-bean soup with fetta toasts

200 g dried lima beans

2 tablespoons olive oil

750 g lamb shanks

1 clove garlic, finely chopped

2 medium-sized brown onions, diced

2 medium-sized carrots, peeled and diced

2 cups chicken stock (page 15)

1 litre water

400 g canned chopped tomatoes

2 tablespoons freshly squeezed lemon juice

salt and freshly ground black pepper

½ cup torn fresh mint leaves

FETTA TOASTS

8 pieces ciabatta or other rustic-style bread

100 g fetta cheese

Check the beans for impurities, then rinse and place in a bowl, cover with plenty of fresh water and leave to stand overnight. Drain.

Heat oil in a large, heavy-based pan and sauté lamb in batches until well browned. Remove from pan and set aside.

Heat a little more oil in the pan if necessary, add garlic, onions and carrots and cook, stirring, for about 5 minutes. Return lamb to pan, add drained beans, stock and water. Bring to boil, cover, and simmer for about 1 hour. Skim surface occasionally. ➤

Remove lamb shanks from pan. Cool, then remove meat from bones (discard bones), shred the meat and return it to the pan. Add tomatoes, cover pan again and simmer for a further hour.

When beans are cooked, stir the lemon juice through, check seasoning and serve scattered with mint leaves.

To make the fetta toasts, lightly grill or toast the bread, then spread with mashed fetta: serve the toasts on the side.

SERVES 8

Russian borscht

500 g fresh beetroot

1 carrot, peeled and chopped

1 potato, peeled and quartered

1 leek, white part only, sliced

1 onion, quartered

4 tablespoons freshly squeezed
  lemon juice

½ teaspoon ground allspice

½ teaspoon ground nutmeg

1 tablespoon chopped fresh dill

2 bay leaves

1.5 litres beef stock

salt and freshly ground
  black pepper

1 cup sour cream

extra chopped fresh dill,
  to serve

Wash, trim and peel beetroot, and cut into chunks (wear rubber gloves to avoid staining your fingers).

Place beetroot, carrot, potato, leek, onion, lemon juice, spices, dill and bay leaves in a large saucepan with the stock. Bring to the boil, reduce the heat, partially cover and simmer for 2 hours, stirring occasionally.

Allow soup to cool a little, then blend in batches until smooth. Season well with salt and freshly ground pepper. Return to saucepan and gently reheat.

Serve with a dollop of sour cream and a sprinkling of fresh dill.

SERVES 6

Scotch broth

½ cup pearl barley

1 kg lamb shanks (or necks),
   cut into 5-cm lengths
   (ask your butcher to do this)

2 onions, chopped

1 bay leaf

1 sprig fresh thyme

2 litres water

1 carrot, peeled and cut into
   thick slices

1 turnip, finely chopped

1 leek, white part only, finely
   sliced

1 stick celery, cut into thick slices

salt and freshly ground
   black pepper

½ cup chopped flat-leaf parsley

Rinse pearl barley, place in a bowl, cover with boiling water and soak for 1 hour. Drain.

Place lamb, onions, bay leaf, thyme and water in a large saucepan. Cover, bring just to the boil, then reduce heat and simmer for about 1 hour. Check occasionally, skimming the surface to remove scum. Transfer the meat to a plate and leave to cool, then remove meat from the bones.

Skim any fat from the surface of the broth, remove the bay leaf and thyme. Return meat to broth and add the carrot, turnip, leek, celery and pearl barley. Simmer on a very low heat for another hour. Check for seasoning adding salt and freshly ground pepper to taste. Stir fresh parsley through the soup before serving.

SERVES 4

Sunday-night lentil & ham soup

2 tablespoons vegetable oil

2 cloves garlic, crushed

1 medium-sized brown onion, finely diced

2 medium-sized stalks celery, finely sliced

2 medium-sized carrots, peeled and diced

400 g brown lentils, rinsed and drained

600 g ham hock

3 litres water

2 bay leaves

2 tablespoons finely chopped flat-leaf parsley

Heat oil in a large, heavy-based saucepan. Add garlic, onion, celery and carrots, and cook, stirring, for about 5 minutes, or until onion is soft. Add lentils, ham hock, water and bay leaves, and bring to boil. Reduce heat, cover and simmer for about 1 hour, until lentils are tender. Stir occasionally and skim the surface.

Remove ham hock and bay leaves from the pan. Discard skin from ham and slice the meat into small pieces.

Allow the soup to cool a little, then blend in batches until smooth. Return soup to pot, add meat and gently reheat.

Sprinkle with parsley and serve with plenty of crusty fresh bread.

SERVES 6

Tuscan lentil soup

250 g brown lentils

1 onion, chopped

1 stalk celery, chopped

1 carrot, peeled and chopped

2 litres chicken or
  vegetable stock

2 cloves garlic, finely chopped

6 anchovies, rinsed and
  finely chopped

2 tablespoons chopped
  flat-leaf parsley

6 fresh sage leaves

100 ml good-quality olive oil

12 black peppercorns, roughly
  crushed

Put the lentils in a large pot with the onion, celery, carrot and stock. Bring to the boil, then simmer for about 1 hour or until vegetables are tender. Towards the end of the cooking time, remove lid so that the liquid reduces a little.

Remove pot from the heat and add the garlic, anchovies, parsley, sage and peppercorns. Stir to combine, then leave to stand for at least an hour, to allow flavours to mingle. Reheat, and serve.

SERVES 4–6

Seafood

For many people, a seafood meal is a quick-grilled fillet of fish, or a few prawns tossed on the barbecue. But slow-cooked seafood is a tradition of Mediterranean and Middle Eastern cultures, among others, and is a wonderful way to enjoy our bounty of superb fresh seafood.

Slow cooking is the perfect way to prepare seafood when you are catering for a large number of guests, or need to prepare your meal ahead of time. You can bake a whole fish, for example, the long cooking process releasing subtle flavours and producing tender and juicy flesh. You can simmer generous portions of seafood in a stew rich with tomato and garlic, and laced with wine, which imparts complex flavours and rich colour. Salted and smoked fish can be converted into creamy, delicate purées such as the brandade of salt cod on page 42. The possibilities really are endless.

❮ Brandade of salt cod (page 42)

Brandade of salt cod

500 g salt cod

2 cups milk

4 black peppercorns

2 sprigs fresh parsley

2 bay leaves

2 cloves garlic, chopped

juice of 1 lemon

1 cup olive oil

750 g floury potatoes, steamed, peeled and mashed

3 tablespoons chopped flat-leaf parsley

freshly ground black pepper

Place salt cod in a bowl, cover with cold water and leave to soak (in refrigerator) for 48 hours. Change the water twice a day, to remove excess salt and rehydrate the fish. Drain cod and rinse again before starting the recipe.

Place prepared cod in a large saucepan with milk, peppercorns, parsley and bay leaves and enough water to cover fish. Poach gently for 15–20 minutes or until the fish is soft and flaky. Remove carefully from the pan (reserve about 3 tablespoons of the poaching liquid) drain, and cool. Flake fish and discard bones and skin. Be sure there are no small bones left.

Put fish into a blender or food processor with the garlic and half the lemon juice. Turn on blender and drizzle in the oil, blending until you have a thick purée.

Add potatoes and parsley, and pulse a few times until ingredients are just combined. Add a little of the reserved poaching liquid if mixture is too stiff, then season with freshly ground pepper. The mixture should be creamy and light.

Serve at room temperature with toast or crispbreads. Brandade will keep (refrigerated) for 2–3 days.

 This creamy, subtly flavoured purée is a traditional favourite in Mediterranean Spain and France. Salt cod (which has been dried and then salted) is available from Italian and Spanish food stores, and produce markets.

SERVES 6

Dalmatian fish stew

1 kg mixed fish (e.g. salmon, tuna, John Dory)

½ cup olive oil

1 onion, chopped

2 tablespoons chopped flat-leaf parsley

2 cloves garlic, crushed

salt and freshly ground black pepper

2 ripe tomatoes, thickly sliced

2 tablespoons tomato paste

2 tablespoons wine vinegar

soft polenta (page 208), or pasta, to serve

Cut larger fish into thick slices or chunks, and leave any smaller fish whole.

Heat oil in a heavy-based saucepan over medium heat, add onion and sauté for 2–3 minutes until just soft. Add garlic and parsley, stir for 1 minute, then add fish pieces and cook for a few minutes until just lightly browned on all sides. Season with salt and freshly ground pepper, then add tomatoes and tomato paste.

Pour in just enough water to cover fish, increase heat and bring to the boil. Stir in vinegar, reduce heat to very low, cover and simmer for 1–1½ hours. Do not stir, but gently shake pan to keep fish covered with liquid, if needed. Check seasoning.

Serve with polenta or pasta to soak up the juices.

SERVES 4

Moroccan fish tagine with chermoula

4 × 180-g white-fleshed fish
   steaks (e.g. swordfish)

1 tablespoon olive oil

250 g floury potatoes, peeled
   and thickly sliced

salt and freshly ground
   black pepper

2 green capsicums, deseeded
   and thinly sliced

500 g ripe tomatoes, sliced

½ cup tomato passata
   (see note page 73)

2 tablespoons finely chopped
   fresh coriander

2 tablespoons finely chopped
   flat-leaf parsley

couscous or polenta, to serve

CHERMOULA

1½ cups chopped fresh coriander

1½ cups chopped flat-leaf
   parsley

4 cloves garlic, crushed

1 teaspoon ground sweet paprika

¼ teaspoon ground cayenne

½ teaspoon cumin seeds,
   roasted and ground

1 small onion, roughly chopped

2 tablespoons freshly squeezed
   lemon juice

½ cup extra-virgin olive oil

pinch of ground cinnamon

1 teaspoon freshly ground
   black pepper

1 teaspoon sea salt

To make chermoula, place all ingredients in blender and process to a thick paste. Leave for 1 hour at least, for flavours to develop.   **>**

Place fish steaks in a bowl, cover with half the chermoula and put in refrigerator to marinate for 2–3 hours.

Preheat oven to 200°C. Lightly oil an ovenproof tagine (or you can use an earthenware or enamelled casserole dish). Place potato slices in the dish and season with salt and freshly ground pepper. Place fish steaks on top, then a layer of capsicum slices and a layer of tomato. Spread a little chermoula over, pour in tomato passata, sprinkle with chopped coriander and parsley, and season again. Finally spread the remainder of the chermoula over the top. Cover, place in preheated oven and bake for 1 hour or until fish and potatoes are tender.

Serve with couscous (page 192) or soft polenta (page 208).

 Chermoula is traditionally used as a marinade for fish, but it also goes well with chicken. Add a small amount of fresh chilli if you like a little extra heat. This recipe for chermoula makes 1 cup.

SERVES 4

Octopus braised
with tomatoes & red wine

2 kg octopus, cleaned and beak
    removed (ask your fishmonger
    to do this)

¾ cup olive oil

500 g shallots or small pickling
    onions

1 cup red wine

400 g canned chopped tomatoes

1 clove garlic, crushed

1 cinnamon stick

2 bay leaves

1 tablespoon red wine vinegar

freshly ground black pepper

chopped flat-leaf parsley,
    to serve

Rinse the cleaned octopus well. Place in a pot and cover with boiling water. Bring back to the boil and simmer for 10 minutes. Remove from the pot and drain.

When octopus is cool enough to handle, rub under running water to remove the dark outer membrane. Cut body and tentacles into 5-cm pieces.

Heat olive oil in large heavy-based saucepan over medium heat, then add onions and octopus and sauté for 5–6 minutes, stirring. Add wine and cook for 5 minutes, stirring occasionally. Add chopped tomatoes, garlic, cinnamon and bay leaves, and a little water if needed to cover octopus. Bring just to the boil, then reduce heat to very low, cover and simmer for 45–60 minutes, stirring occasionally and adding a little extra water or wine if there is not enough sauce. **>**

When octopus is tender, add vinegar and freshly ground pepper, stir well and cook for 1–2 minutes. Remove from heat and leave to sit for 10 minutes.

Sprinkle with parsley and serve.

SERVES 4–6

Salt-baked ocean trout

4 egg whites

3 kg cooking salt

2.5 kg whole ocean trout

350 g fresh rocket leaves

rosemary potatoes (page 217) and
    salsa verde (page 218), to serve

Preheat oven to 180°C.

Place egg whites in a medium-sized bowl, beat very lightly with a fork to break them up, then mix in salt. Spread about half the salt mix over the base of a large roasting pan or baking dish. Wipe down fish with paper towel, then place fish on salt mix and cover with remaining mixture, leaving just the tail uncovered.

Place baking dish in preheated oven and bake for 1 hour. Remove fish from oven and use a heavy knife to break the salt crust (be careful not to cut through the fish). Transfer fish to a serving plate, remove skin and slice fish into serving pieces.

Arrange rocket on individual plates with the potatoes. Place fish pieces on top and serve salsa verde separately.

SERVES 6

Chicken, duck & rabbit

While a quick-grilled fillet of chicken or duck undoubtedly makes for an easy meal, slow-cooking poultry opens up an entirely different world of flavour.

When buying chicken for slow-cooking, don't choose expensive breast fillets — they tend to dry out or become tough. A whole chicken, or thighs, wings and drumsticks, are preferable, as the bone and muscle will give the dish much more flavour. For the same reason, opt for certified organic or free-range chicken, which has benefited from both exercise and a better diet.

Duck responds wonderfully to slow cooking. Its dark, rich meat and natural fats are perfect for slow-roasting and braising, resulting in tender meat and a full-bodied sauce.

Rabbit (especially wild rabbit) is lean and low-fat, but lends itself beautifully to slow-cooking. Marinated beforehand, the meat will be even more succulent and flavoursome.

< Basque chicken (page 56)

Basque chicken

2 tablespoons Spanish olive oil

1.5 kg free-range chicken
pieces on the bone
(e.g. maryland pieces)

2 garlic cloves, finely chopped

1 red onion, chopped

1 red capsicum, deseeded
and cut in thick slices

1 green capsicum, deseeded
and cut in thick slices

1 small fresh red chilli,
deseeded and cut in
thick slices

1 sprig fresh rosemary

1 bay leaf

½ cup dry white wine

2 ripe tomatoes, peeled
and chopped

2 tablespoons tomato paste

1½ cups chicken stock

60 g good-quality pitted olives

salt and freshly ground
black pepper

2 tablespoons chopped
flat-leaf parsley

Preheat oven to 220°C.

Heat the oil in a heavy-based saucepan and sauté chicken pieces in
batches until golden-brown all over. Remove them from the pan and
set aside.

Add garlic, onion, capsicums, chilli, rosemary, bay leaf and wine to
the pan. Bring slowly to the boil, then boil until reduced by half.

Add the tomatoes, tomato paste and chicken stock, stir and then bring to the boil, skimming the surface. Reduce heat to a slow simmer, return the chicken pieces to the pan and add the olives. Cover and simmer for 50–60 minutes.

To serve, season to taste with salt and pepper, and sprinkle with fresh parsley.

SERVES 4

Chicken baked in Thai green curry

2½ cups coconut milk

3 tablespoons Thai fish sauce
(nam pla)

juice of 1 lemon

2 tablespoons torn fresh
Thai basil leaves

3 kaffir lime leaves, torn

2 kg free-range chicken pieces
(e.g. thighs, drumsticks)

4 fresh green bird's-eye chillies,
split in half and deseeded

4 cardamom pods

10 black peppercorns

1 teaspoon coriander seeds

½ red onion, chopped

¾ cup chopped fresh
coriander leaves

½ cup chopped fresh
mint leaves

grated zest and juice of 1 lime

1 × 5-cm piece fresh galangal,
peeled and chopped

1 × 5-cm piece fresh lemongrass,
outer leaves peeled away, and
flesh chopped

1 tablespoon cumin seeds

1 teaspoon ground turmeric

2 cloves garlic, chopped

1 teaspoon shrimp paste
(blachan)

sea salt

2 tablespoons olive oil

extra fresh coriander leaves,
to serve

Make a marinade by putting coconut milk, fish sauce, lemon juice, basil and two of the lime leaves in a small bowl and whisking until combined. Place chicken pieces in a non-metallic bowl. Pour the marinade over, coat chicken pieces well, cover bowl tightly with plastic wrap and refrigerate overnight.

Preheat oven to 135°C.

Place chillies, cardamom pods, peppercorns, coriander seeds and remaining lime leaf in a spice grinder, and grind to a fine powder.

Place onion, coriander leaves, mint leaves, lime zest and juice, galangal, lemongrass, cumin seeds, turmeric, garlic and shrimp paste in a blender. Blend to make a thick paste, and season with salt to taste.

Remove chicken pieces from the marinade (reserve marinade for later) and pat dry. Heat oil over high heat in a medium-sized flameproof casserole dish. Sauté chicken pieces, in batches, for 5–6 minutes until golden-brown. Transfer chicken to a plate. Reduce the heat, add onion and spice mixtures and cook, stirring, for 3–4 minutes. Pour in reserved marinade and bring to a simmer.

Return chicken to the casserole, and cover. Place the dish in preheated oven and cook for 1¼ hours.

Serve with steamed fragrant rice, scattered with fresh coriander leaves.

SERVES 4

Chicken chasseur, slow-simmered

1 tablespoon olive oil

1.5 kg free-range chicken pieces
(legs and thighs as well as
breast on the bone)

200 g button mushrooms, halved

½ cup dry white wine

3 tablespoons brandy or cognac

2 cups chicken stock

3 tablespoons tomato paste

1 tablespoon chopped fresh
flat-leaf parsley

1 tablespoon chopped fresh
tarragon

salt and freshly ground
black pepper

extra fresh tarragon, to serve

Heat oil in a large, heavy-based frying pan. Cook chicken in batches until golden-brown, then drain on paper towel.

Pour excess fat from pan, leaving about 1 tablespoon. Add mushrooms and cook over medium heat until they start to brown. Add wine, brandy, stock, tomato paste and herbs, and bring to boil. Return chicken pieces to the pan, cover and simmer for 1¼ hours, stirring occasionally.

Season with salt and freshly ground pepper and scatter over fresh tarragon before serving.

SERVES 6

Chicken tagine

6 chicken thighs

6 chicken legs

4 tablespoons olive oil

4 red onions, chopped

4 cloves garlic, crushed

½ cup chopped flat-leaf parsley

½ cup ras al hanout
  (see note below)

½ teaspoon saffron threads

salt and freshly ground
  black pepper

1 cup chicken stock

chopped rind of 2 preserved
  lemons (page 211)

½ cup chilli-marinated olives

couscous (page 192), to serve

Place chicken pieces, oil, onions, garlic, parsley, ras al hanout, saffron, salt and freshly ground pepper in a large bowl and mix to coat chicken. Leave to marinate for 2–3 hours, or overnight.

Place chicken and marinade in a large saucepan or tagine. Add chicken stock, bring to boil, cover and simmer for 1¼ hours. Add extra stock if needed, and the olives and preserved lemon. Cook for a further 15 minutes and check seasoning before serving with couscous.

 Ras al hanout is a Moroccan mix of spices and aromatics that contains up to 25 ingredients. It can be bought at Middle Eastern food stores and good delis.

SERVES 6

Chicken, mushroom & thyme braise

100 g prosciutto, cut into strips

50 g butter

2 medium-sized leeks, white part only, finely sliced

2 cloves garlic, crushed

1 tablespoon chopped fresh thyme

1.5 kg free-range chicken pieces

2 tablespoons plain flour

1½ cups dry white wine

1½ cups chicken stock

350 g button mushrooms, stems trimmed

salt and freshly ground black pepper

¼ cup cream (optional)

steamed jasmine rice, to serve

Preheat oven to 160°C.

Gently dry-fry prosciutto in a heavy-based saucepan for about 2 minutes until starting to brown. Remove from pan and set aside.

Melt half the butter in the same pan. Add leeks, garlic and thyme, and cook, stirring occasionally, until the leeks are soft. Remove and set aside.

Dip chicken pieces in flour and dust off any excess. Put remaining butter in the pan and melt over medium–high heat. Cook the chicken pieces in batches, turning to make sure they are brown on all sides. Remove chicken and set aside.

Pour wine into the pan and bring to the boil. Cook over high heat for about 1 minute, stirring to release any residue. Add stock and button mushrooms, and stir.

Place leek mixture and chicken pieces in a casserole dish and pour the sauce and mushrooms over. Cover, place in preheated oven and cook for 1 hour, or until chicken is tender.

When cooked, use a spoon to skim any excess fat from the surface. Add cream, if using, and stir to combine.

Serve with steamed jasmine rice.

SERVES 4−6

Coq au vin

2 kg free-range chicken pieces

60 g plain flour, seasoned with salt and pepper

1 tablespoon olive oil

1 tablespoon butter

2 cloves garlic, finely chopped

12 shallots or small pickling onions, peeled but left whole

200 g bacon, chopped

1 sprig thyme

1 bay leaf

2 cups chicken stock

2 cups red wine

3 tablespoons cognac or brandy

250 g button mushrooms

extra salt and freshly ground black pepper

Dust chicken pieces with seasoned flour and shake off any excess. Heat oil and butter in wide heavy-based frying pan (or flameproof casserole dish) and sauté chicken in batches, turning often until pieces are well browned on all sides. Place chicken on paper towel to drain.

Add garlic, shallots and bacon to pan and cook until shallots are lightly browned. Place chicken pieces back in the pan and add thyme and bay leaf.

Warm cognac in a small saucepan, then pour it over chicken. When flames die down, add chicken stock and wine and bring to boil. Reduce heat until sauce is simmering, cover and then cook over low heat for about 1 hour, stirring occasionally.

Add the mushrooms to the pan, check for seasoning and add extra salt and black pepper if needed, then simmer for another 10 minutes.

If there is too much liquid, remove chicken pieces and boil the sauce for a few minutes until reduced, then return chicken to the pan.

 Traditionally a rooster (*coq*) was used for this dish, slow-cooked until it was impregnated with the wine sauce, the flavours rich and deep. If you prefer, buy a whole chicken and cut into pieces.

SERVES 6

Duck braised with pink peppercorns

2 tablespoons olive oil

3 duck maryland pieces

3 duck breasts

15 shallots or small pickling onions

4 cloves garlic, peeled but left whole

4 sprigs fresh thyme

3 bay leaves

4 teaspoons pink peppercorns (see note page 70)

3½ cups chicken or vegetable stock

½ cup dry white wine

salt and freshly ground black pepper

creamy mash (page 194), to serve

Preheat oven to 180°C.

Heat oil over a high heat in a large, flameproof casserole dish, add duck pieces in batches and cook for 4–5 minutes, or until golden-brown. Transfer duck to a plate and set aside. Pour off any excess fat, leaving about 1 tablespoon in the dish.

Reduce heat, add shallots and garlic to casserole, and cook for 3–4 minutes, until the vegetables start to brown. Return duck to the dish, add thyme, bay leaves, peppercorns, stock and wine, and season with salt and freshly ground pepper. Cover and bake in preheated oven for 1½ hours, until duck is tender.   **>**

Before serving, remove bay leaves and thyme sprigs and skim any excess fat from the surface.

Serve with creamy mashed potatoes. A bitter salad (e.g. of radicchio leaves) goes well with this dish, cutting the richness of the duck.

 Pink peppercorns are not true peppercorns but the dried fruit of a type of rose, which add a spicy, peppery flavour. They are available at gourmet delis and some supermarkets.

SERVES 6

Duck ragu with pappardelle

1 tablespoon olive oil

4 duck maryland pieces

150 g bacon, chopped

1 brown onion, finely chopped

2 cloves garlic, crushed

1 carrot, peeled and finely sliced

2 stalks celery, finely sliced

½ cup chopped flat-leaf parsley

4–5 fresh sage leaves, chopped

1 cup dry white wine

2 cups tomato passata
  (see note page 73)

pinch of freshly grated nutmeg

1 bay leaf

½ cup boiling water
  or chicken stock

salt and freshly ground pepper

pappardelle pasta, to serve

Preheat oven to 220°C.

Heat oil in a large flameproof casserole over medium heat. Add duck, skin-side down, and cook for 8–10 minutes until skin is golden and most of the fat has been released. Turn and cook for 3–4 minutes on the other side, then transfer to a plate.

Add bacon to casserole and fry for 2–3 minutes, or until crisp and golden. Use a slotted spoon to transfer to a plate. Drain off excess fat, leaving about 1 tablespoon in the casserole dish.

Add onion, garlic, carrot, celery, parsley and sage to the casserole dish, increase the heat to high and stir for 2–3 minutes until vegetables are **>**

starting to soften. Add wine and bring to the boil, then reduce heat to medium.

Return duck to the dish and add cooked bacon, tomato passata, nutmeg and bay leaf. Pour in just enough water or stock to cover the duck and bring to the boil again. Cover dish, place in preheated oven, reduce heat to 160°C and cook for 1½ –1¾ hours, or until the meat is falling off the bone.

Remove from oven and leave to cool. Remove duck from casserole dish, discard skin and bones, shred meat into small pieces and return to the casserole. Reheat slowly, skim off any fat from the surface and season the ragu with salt and freshly ground pepper.

Serve with pappardelle pasta.

 Tomato passata is simply a sieved purée of tomatoes, usually sold in bottles (sometimes labelled 'tomato purée') and available in most supermarkets.

SERVES 6

Farmer's Dijon rabbit

1 rabbit (about 750 g), cut into serving pieces (ask your butcher to do this)

2 tablespoons flour, seasoned with salt and pepper

2 tablespoons olive oil

2 thick slices bacon, cut into strips

1 large onion, sliced

2 cloves garlic, finely chopped

2 teaspoons Dijon mustard

1¼ cups dry white wine

1 tablespoon tomato passata (see note page 73)

1 bay leaf

salt and freshly ground pepper

MARINADE

1 cup red wine

1 cup red wine vinegar

1 clove garlic, chopped

1 sprig fresh rosemary

1 sprig flat-leaf parsley

Put the marinade ingredients in a bowl, add the rabbit pieces, cover, place in the refrigerator and marinate for several hours or overnight.

Preheat the oven to 180°C.

Remove the rabbit pieces from the marinade, pat dry with kitchen paper and dust with the seasoned flour.

Heat olive oil in a non-stick frying pan, add the rabbit a few pieces at time and sauté until browned all over. Transfer to a casserole dish. Add the bacon, onion and garlic to the pan, and cook for a few minutes until softened.   ➤

Add mustard, wine, tomato passata and bay leaf, and season with salt and freshly ground pepper. Bring the liquid to the boil and simmer for 5 minutes. Pour over the rabbit pieces in the casserole dish, cover and bake in the preheated oven for about 1½ hours until rabbit is tender.

 If you use wild rabbit, it will have darker meat and the dish will have a gamier flavour, but farmed rabbit works perfectly well.

SERVES 2–3

Jerez chicken with orange

1 tablespoon Spanish olive oil

6 chicken maryland pieces
  (about 1.3 kg)

1 brown onion, finely chopped

1 medium-sized carrot, peeled
  and finely chopped

1 bay leaf

½ cup dry sherry

3 teaspoons orange zest

¾ cup fresh orange juice,
  strained

1 cup chicken stock

1 small orange, peeled, pith
  removed and flesh cut into
  small cubes

1 cup pimiento-stuffed green
  olives, drained

chopped fresh flat-leaf parsley,
  to serve

Preheat oven to 180°C.

Heat oil in a large heavy-based frying pan over medium–high heat and
sauté chicken in batches, for about 5–6 minutes, until golden-brown.
Transfer chicken to a large roasting dish.

Pour off excess oil, leaving about 2 tablespoons in the pan. Lower heat,
add onion and sauté until softening and just brown. Add carrot and bay
leaf, and cook, stirring occasionally, for about 8 minutes until softened.

Pour in sherry and cook for 1 minute, then add orange zest, juice and stock.
Bring to the boil, stirring well to scrape any residue from the pan. Pour sauce
mixture over the chicken pieces, place roasting dish in preheated oven and
bake for 1–1¼ hours, or until cooked and well coloured. **>**

Remove dish from the oven and pour juices into a small saucepan. Cover chicken and keep warm. Remove any oil from surface of cooking juices, then bring juices to the boil and simmer for 15–20 minutes until sauce thickens and reduces.

Pour sauce over chicken and then sprinkle with the orange cubes and olives. Return chicken to the oven, uncovered and bake for about 10 minutes.

To serve, scatter with parsley.

SERVES 6

Persian chicken with walnuts & pomegranate

3 tablespoons olive oil

1.5 kg free-range chicken pieces, skin removed

1 large brown onion, sliced

½ teaspoon ground turmeric

400 g walnut pieces, lightly toasted and finely chopped

½ cup pomegranate molasses (see note page 81)

freshly ground black pepper

4 cups chicken stock

125 ml freshly squeezed lemon juice

2 tablespoons honey

salt

steamed basmati rice and fresh pomegranate seeds, to serve

In a heavy-based saucepan or frying pan, heat 2 tablespoons of the oil and sauté the chicken pieces in batches until browned all over. Transfer to a plate.

Add the remaining tablespoon of oil to the pan over a medium heat, then add onion and turmeric and sauté until soft. Add chopped walnuts, pomegranate molasses, black pepper and stock, then bring to the boil. Add the sautéed chicken pieces, then reduce heat and simmer on very low, uncovered, for about 1–1¼ hours hour, stirring occasionally.

When chicken is tender and sauce is quite thick, add lemon juice and honey, stir, and continue cooking for another minute until flavours are combined. Check for seasoning and add a little salt and more pepper if needed.

Serve with steamed basmati rice, sprinkled with fresh pomegranate seeds.

 Pomegranate molasses is available from Middle Eastern food suppliers and gourmet food stores. If fresh pomegranates are unavailable, you can substitute dried barberries (available from the same suppliers as the molasses) or cranberries for the pomegranate seeds.

SERVES 6

Rabbit with pancetta & basil

750 g boned rabbit, cut into even-sized chunks

2 cloves garlic, thinly sliced

120 g thinly sliced pancetta

750 g tomatoes

3 tablespoons chopped fresh basil

salt and freshly ground black pepper

60 ml olive oil

soft polenta (page 208), to serve

Preheat oven to 200°C.

Pat the rabbit pieces dry with a paper towel. Place a slice of garlic on each piece of meat, then wrap in a slice of pancetta to make small 'parcels'.

Peel, seed and roughly chop the tomatoes. Put them in a medium-sized saucepan and cook for about 7–8 minutes, until they start to form a sauce. Stir in the basil, and season with salt and freshly ground pepper.

Spoon tomato sauce into base of an ovenproof casserole dish. Place rabbit parcels on top, in a single layer. Place casserole, uncovered, in preheated oven and roast for about 50 minutes, basting occasionally.

After about 30 minutes, if the sauce seems to be drying out too much, cover the dish with aluminium foil.

Serve this dish straight from the casserole, accompanied by soft polenta.

Pancetta is an Italian-style bacon, often sold in wafer-thin slices. If you can't find it, substitute thinly sliced bacon.

SERVES 4

Saffron & fennel chicken

2 onions, quartered

3 cloves garlic, crushed

4 ripe tomatoes, peeled
and quartered

4 small fennel bulbs, trimmed
and cut in thick slices

3 tablespoons olive oil

3 tablespoons Pernod

3 fresh bay leaves

4–5 saffron threads

salt and freshly ground
black pepper

4 chicken maryland pieces,
skin removed

500 g potatoes, peeled
and quartered

2 cups chicken stock

chopped fennel fronds, to serve

Place onions, garlic, tomatoes, fennel, olive oil, Pernod, bay leaves, saffron, salt and freshly ground pepper in a large bowl. Stir well to mix. Add chicken and stir to coat. Cover well and refrigerate overnight or for at least 8 hours.

Remove chicken from the refrigerator an hour before cooking, to bring back to room temperature. Place chicken and marinade in a large, heavy-based saucepan and bring to the boil. Reduce heat, partially cover and simmer for about 40 minutes, stirring occasionally.

Add potatoes and chicken stock, and simmer for another 30 minutes, until potatoes are tender. Check for seasoning, sprinkle with the feathery fennel fronds, and serve.

SERVES 4

Slow-roasted duck with dark cherry sauce

1½ tablespoons olive oil

1 brown onion, halved and thinly sliced

1 cup soft breadcrumbs

60 g pecans, lightly toasted and roughly chopped

100 g whole dried figs, chopped

2 teaspoons fresh thyme leaves

salt and freshly ground black pepper

1 duck (about 2 kg), patted dry inside and out

DARK CHERRY SAUCE

300 g frozen cherries, thawed

2 tablespoons brown sugar

2 tablespoons dry red wine

1 tablespoon cider vinegar

1 bay leaf

1 whole clove

2 whole allspice

To make the stuffing, heat 1 tablespoon of the oil in a non-stick frying pan over medium heat. Add onion and cook for 5–6 minutes until soft. Remove from heat, add breadcrumbs, pecans, figs and thyme, and mix well. Season with salt and freshly ground pepper.

To make the cherry sauce, place all the ingredients in a small saucepan over medium heat. Bring to the boil, then reduce heat and simmer for about 8 minutes, stirring occasionally, until sauce thickens a little.

Preheat oven to 180°C. ➤

Fill the duck cavity with prepared stuffing and tie the legs together with string. Place duck in a roasting pan, breast-side up. Drizzle a little oil over the duck, season with salt and pepper, place in preheated oven and roast for 1 hour. Remove from oven and drain away any excess fat. Reduce oven temperature to 150°C and cook duck for a further 1½ hours until skin is crispy and juices run clear. Remove from oven, cover loosely with aluminium foil and leave in a warm place to rest for 10 minutes.

To serve, cut duck in half along backbone, remove stuffing, then cut into 8 pieces.

Serve with the stuffing and warmed cherry sauce alongside.

 To test if duck (or chicken) is cooked, pierce the thickest part of the thigh with a skewer to see if juices run clear. When you drain duck fat from the pan, strain carefully and keep aside to refrigerate or freeze – it makes crisp and delicious sautéed or roast potatoes.

SERVES 4

Tuscan sage chicken with soft polenta

100 ml olive oil

1.5 kg free-range chicken pieces
(e.g. legs and breast on the bone),
skin removed

salt and freshly ground black pepper

4 cloves garlic, crushed

200 g dry-cured black olives

about 20 fresh sage leaves

½ cup dry white wine

soft polenta (page 208), to serve

Preheat oven to 180°C.

Heat oil in a heavy-based frying pan. Add chicken pieces and cook for about 15 minutes, turning, until golden-brown all over. Season with salt and freshly ground pepper. Add garlic, olives, sage leaves and wine and cook, stirring, for 2–3 minutes.

Transfer chicken pieces and sauce to a casserole dish. Place, uncovered, in preheated oven and roast for about 45 minutes, until chicken is quite tender.

Serve with soft polenta.

Beef, lamb, pork & veal

When the weather cools down, the days are shorter and you yearn for a hearty, comforting meal, a casserole or lovingly prepared slow roast fills the bill perfectly. And, of course, it can be simmering away while you are busy doing other things.

Again, the cheaper cuts — such as shanks and well-muscled meat from the leg, shoulder or ribs — are ideal for this type of cooking: oven-braised, slow-roasted, or simmered on the stove-top, these cuts both soak up the flavours of the sauce and enrich the dish with dense goodness.

The secret is patience — cook low and slow, until time works its magic. There's a long tradition of this peasant-style cook-ing for a reason — because it extracts every ounce of flavour and moisture from the ingredients. And the results are not only delicious but also melt-in-the-mouth tender.

< Afghani lamb with chickpeas, mint & yoghurt
(page 92)

Afghani lamb with chickpeas, mint & yoghurt

225 g dried chickpeas

3 tablespoons olive oil

1 kg boned lamb leg, cut into 6-cm cubes

3 tablespoons olive oil

2 onions, thinly sliced

1 clove garlic, crushed

2½ cups water

½ teaspoon ground turmeric

½ teaspoon ground paprika

2 tablespoons chopped fresh mint

salt and freshly ground black pepper

500 g potatoes, peeled and quartered

1 tablespoon freshly squeezed lemon juice

steamed rice and fresh mint leaves, to serve

YOGHURT SAUCE

1 clove garlic, crushed

1 cup plain yoghurt

Soak the chickpeas in plenty of cold water overnight. Drain.

Heat oil in a large non-stick pan over medium heat, add lamb in batches and sauté for 5–6 minutes, turning until browned on all sides. Transfer to a plate and set aside.

Add onion and garlic to the pan and cook for a few minutes until softened. Return the meat to the pan, add the drained chickpeas and the water, and bring to the boil (skim the surface to remove any scum). Add the spices and mint, season with salt and freshly ground pepper, reduce heat to low, cover and simmer for 1 hour.

After this time, add potatoes and lemon juice, and some more water if needed. Simmer for another 30 minutes, until meat is very tender and potatoes are cooked.

To make yoghurt sauce, simply mix the garlic into the yoghurt and season with salt.

Serve this dish with steamed rice, scattered with mint leaves. Serve the yoghurt sauce on the side.

SERVES 4

Beef rendang

3 tablespoons vegetable oil

1.5 kg stewing beef, cut into
  4-cm cubes

2 cups coconut milk

salt

steamed jasmine rice, to serve

RENDANG SPICE PASTE

6 small fresh red chillies,
  deseeded and sliced

½ onion, chopped

1 × 5-cm piece fresh ginger,
  peeled and chopped

3 cloves garlic, finely chopped

1 stalk lemongrass, outer leaves
  removed, soft stem chopped

3 tablespoons tamarind
  concentrate (see note page 95)

1 teaspoon ground turmeric

1 teaspoon ground coriander

1 teaspoon ground cumin

1 teaspoon ground fennel seeds

pinch of freshly grated nutmeg

1 cup warm water

To make the spice paste, put everything in a blender and whiz to a purée.

Heat oil in a heavy-based, non-stick saucepan and sauté beef for
4–5 minutes, in batches, until golden-brown. Pour spice paste over beef,
then stir in the coconut milk. Bring slowly to the boil, reduce heat, cover
and simmer for 1–1½ hours, until the meat is tender and the sauce rich and
dark. Season to taste with a little salt, if desired. Check the pan regularly

as the rendang cooks: this curry should be fairly dry, so if you need to add any liquid, only add a very small amount.

Serve with steamed jasmine rice.

 Tamarind concentrate is available in jars from Asian food stores. It is best mixed with warm water before being added to a dish.

SERVES 6–8

Beef with apricots

1 tablespoon vegetable oil

400 g lean stewing beef, cut into 6-cm cubes

salt and freshly ground black pepper

2 brown onions, chopped

3 cloves garlic, crushed

100 g dried apricots, halved

50 g semi-dried tomatoes, chopped

400 g canned chopped tomatoes

600 ml water

creamy mash (page 194) and freshly grated nutmeg, to serve

Heat oil in a heavy-based, non-stick pan. Sauté beef in batches until well browned on all sides. Season with salt and freshly ground pepper, then set aside.

Add onions and garlic to pan and sauté for 5–6 minutes, stirring, until soft. Return beef to the pan and add apricots, semi-dried and canned tomatoes, and water. Bring to the boil, cover and simmer for 1–1¼ hours, stirring occasionally.

Serve with creamy mash dusted with freshly grated nutmeg.

SERVES 4

Boeuf bourguignon

1 kg beef blade or chuck steak, trimmed of fat and cut into 3-cm cubes

2 cups red wine

1 teaspoon chopped fresh thyme

2 cloves garlic, chopped

1 bay leaf

2 teaspoons plain flour

1 tablespoon olive oil

200 g bacon, cut into strips

200 g button mushrooms

300 g shallots or small pickling onions

1 cup beef stock

salt and freshly ground black pepper

Place beef, wine, thyme, garlic and bay leaf in a bowl, cover and marinate for 2–3 hours, or overnight if possible.

Preheat oven to 140°C.

Remove meat from marinade, drain, pat dry and dust with flour. Reserve marinade.

Heat oil in a flameproof casserole dish. Fry bacon for a few minutes until starting to crisp, then transfer to a plate. Fry beef in batches until well browned all over, then transfer to a plate.

Add shallots to the pan and cook, stirring occasionally, for 5–6 minutes until softened. Add mushrooms and cook for a further 5 minutes until mushrooms are just browned.

Return beef to casserole dish. Stir in stock and reserved marinade, and bring to a simmer. Cover and place in preheated oven and cook for 2 hours.

After this time, add cooked shallots and mushrooms to the dish, stir gently, cover and return to oven for a further 30 minutes, or until meat is very tender. Season with salt and freshly ground pepper if needed.

 This rich dish marries well with steamed chat potatoes tossed with a little butter, some fresh parsley and a twist of freshly ground black pepper.

SERVES 6

Bolognese ragu

2 tablespoons olive oil
1 tablespoon butter
2 cloves garlic, crushed
2 red onions, diced
1 large carrot, peeled and diced
2 stalks celery, diced
1 kg beef mince
500 g pork mince

1 cup milk
salt and freshly ground
   black pepper
freshly grated nutmeg
1 cup dry white wine
400 g canned chopped tomatoes
grated parmesan cheese, to serve

Heat oil and butter over medium heat in a large, non-stick frying pan. Add garlic and onion, and sauté for 4–5 minutes until softened. Add carrot and celery and sauté for a few more minutes, stirring, until they start to soften.

Add meat in batches and sauté until browned all over. Return to pan, season with a little salt, freshly ground pepper and some grated nutmeg, then add milk and continue to cook until the liquid has evaporated. Add white wine and stir again, then cook until the wine has reduced.

Add chopped tomatoes, stir well, then simmer over a very low heat, uncovered, for 2–3 hours. Stir occasionally, adding a little extra water if the sauce is getting too dry.   >

Serve with your favourite pasta, with freshly grated parmesan on the side.

 The secret to a traditional Italian meat ragu is to use more than one type of meat, and allow plenty of time for it to simmer very slowly (you can cook the sauce in a crockpot or slow-cooker on low, for 6–8 hours). This sauce freezes well.

SERVES 6

Carbonnade of beef

6 tablespoons olive oil

1.5 kg beef brisket, trimmed and cut into 2-cm slices

salt and freshly ground black pepper

2 teaspoons muscovado or soft brown sugar

3 tablespoons plain flour

2 cups beer (dark ale or stout is best)

2 cups chicken or beef stock

2 large onions, thinly sliced

2 tablespoons finely chopped fresh thyme leaves

steamed rice, or wide egg noodles, to serve

Heat 3 tablespoons of the oil over high heat in a large frying pan. Add beef pieces in batches and sear on both sides (being careful not to burn), then transfer to a plate.

Add another tablespoon of oil to the pan, add sugar and flour, and whisk to combine. Add beer and stock, and bring to the boil while stirring. Strain liquid into a bowl and set aside.

Heat the remaining 2 tablespoons of oil in the pan, and add onions and 2 tablespoons water. Season with salt and pepper, cover, and cook for about 15 minutes, stirring occasionally, until onions have caramelised.

Preheat oven to 160°C. ➤

Layer beef and onions in a flameproof casserole dish, sprinkling with salt, pepper and thyme, finishing with a layer of meat. Pour reserved beer and stock over meat, then bring to a slow boil over medium heat. Place a piece of buttered baking paper over meat, then cover dish with a lid. Place in preheated oven and bake for 3 hours. Check occasionally (being careful to let the juices from the lid run back into the dish), in case you need to add a little extra water. When cooked, skim any excess fat from the surface.

Serve with steamed rice or wide egg noodles.

 An alternative to baking this in the oven is to leave it in a slow-cooker, on low, for up to 7–8 hours. A carbonnade reheats particularly well, improving in flavour.

SERVES 6

Cassoulet

675 g dried white haricot
(or butter) beans

2 large onions, sliced

4 cloves garlic, crushed

3 bay leaves

3 sprigs fresh thyme

2 cloves

4 tablespoons tomato paste

12 semi-dried tomatoes,
chopped

450 g pancetta (in a piece)

4 tablespoons olive oil

4 boned duck breasts

12 Toulouse pork sausages

400 g canned tomatoes

salt and freshly ground
black pepper

CRUMB CRUST

1½ cups dry breadcrumbs

1 clove garlic, crushed

2 tablespoons flat-leaf parsley

1 tablespoon olive oil

Place dried beans in a large bowl, cover well with cold water and leave to soak overnight. Drain beans, place in a large saucepan, cover with plenty of fresh water and bring to the boil. Boil for 10 minutes, then drain and put into a large flameproof casserole dish. Add onions, garlic, bay leaves, thyme, cloves, tomato paste and semi-dried tomatoes.

Snip rind from pancetta and cut flesh into large chunks. Heat oil in a frying pan and sauté pancetta in batches until browned. Add it to casserole dish and pour in enough water to cover. Bring to the boil, and use a spoon to remove any scum from the surface. Reduce heat, cover and simmer for about 1½ hours until the beans are soft (but not mushy).

Preheat oven to 180°C.

Cut duck breasts and sausages into large pieces. Heat 2 tablespoons of oil in a frying pan and fry duck pieces, skin-side down, until browned, then add to casserole. Fry sausages until golden-brown, then add these to the casserole too. Add tomatoes, salt and freshly ground pepper, and stir to mix.

To make the crust, heat oil and sauté garlic for about 1 minute. Add breadcrumbs, parsley, salt and pepper to the pan, and toss to combine. Sprinkle crumb mix over meat and beans, place dish in preheated oven and bake, uncovered, for 50–60 minutes, until a golden crust has formed.

 There are endless versions of this classic slow-cooked French dish, but white beans, sausages and duck (or goose) and/or pork are traditional ingredients. An authentic cassoulet could take days to make, with some aficionados even making their own sausages.

SERVES 6–8

Chilli con carne with avocado salsa & sour cream

225 g dried red kidney beans

2–3 tablespoons vegetable oil

1 kg beef chuck steak, cut into
  2-cm cubes

1 large brown onion, chopped

2 cloves garlic, finely chopped

1 fresh red chilli, deseeded
  and finely chopped

1 teaspoon ground cumin

1 teaspoon ground coriander

800 g canned chopped tomatoes

½ cup tomato paste

375 ml beef or chicken stock

salt and freshly ground pepper

1 cup sour cream, to serve

AVOCADO SALSA

1 large ripe avocado

1 tablespoon finely chopped
  spring onion

1 tablespoon freshly squeezed
  lime juice

few drops Tabasco sauce

salt

Place kidney beans in a bowl, cover with cold water and soak overnight. Drain and put in a saucepan, cover with fresh water, bring to the boil and simmer for 1 hour or until almost soft. Drain.

Preheat oven to 170°C.

Heat oil over high heat in a large, flameproof casserole dish. Cook beef in batches for 7–8 minutes, until brown all over. Transfer to a plate. **>**

Add onion to casserole and sauté for 5 minutes until softened. Add garlic, chilli, cumin and coriander, and cook for another minute, until fragrant. Return beef to casserole, add tomatoes, beans, tomato paste and stock. Season with pepper, stir well and then bring to a simmer. Cover and place casserole dish in preheated oven and cook for 1½ hours. If the sauce looks too thin, leave the lid off for the last half hour of cooking. When meat is soft and beans cooked, check for seasoning, adding salt and extra pepper if needed.

To make avocado salsa, peel avocado, remove the stone, and then chop flesh into small cubes. Place in a bowl with the spring onion, lime juice, Tabasco and a sprinkle of salt, and stir gently to combine.

To serve, sprinkle chilli con carne with fresh coriander leaves and serve bowls of sour cream and avocado salsa on the side.

 Corn or wheat tortillas, warmed in the oven or char-grilled, are also terrific served with this dish.

SERVES 4−6

Classic beef goulash

750 g stewing beef (e.g. topside or chuck), cut into 6-cm cubes

4–5 tablespoons plain flour, seasoned with salt and pepper

60 g butter

2 tablespoons vegetable oil

1 clove garlic, finely chopped

2 large onions, chopped

1 tablespoon ground paprika

400 g canned chopped tomatoes

2 tablespoons tomato paste

1 cup beef stock

1 bay leaf

salt and freshly ground black pepper

½ cup sour cream

Dust beef with seasoned flour, then shake off any excess. Heat butter and oil in a heavy-based saucepan. Sauté beef in batches, until well browned, then transfer to a plate and set aside.

Add garlic, onion and paprika to the pan and cook, stirring, for a few minutes. Return meat to the pan and add tomatoes, tomato paste, stock and bay leaf and bring just to the boil. Cover, lower heat and simmer for 2 hours until meat is tender. Check occasionally and add extra water if stew is becoming dry.

When meat is cooked, season with salt and freshly ground pepper, then gently stir sour cream through before serving.

SERVES 4–6

Daube of beef
with black-olive tapenade

1.25 kg beef topside or chuck,
    cut into 6-cm cubes

3 tablespoons olive oil

1 onion, chopped

200 g bacon, diced

salt and freshly ground
    black pepper

6 tomatoes, chopped

zest of 1 orange

2 tablespoons good-quality black
    olive tapenade

creamy potato mash, to serve

MARINADE

2 carrots, peeled and sliced

2 onions, roughly chopped

3 cloves garlic, finely chopped

1 sprig fresh thyme

1 sprig fresh rosemary

1 sprig fresh parsley

2 cloves

4–5 black peppercorns

1 bay leaf

750 ml red wine

Mix all marinade ingredients together. Place the meat in a large bowl, pour marinade over, cover and refrigerate overnight. Turn the meat pieces once or twice while marinating.

Heat oil in a heavy-based frying pan over medium heat and sauté onion and bacon until soft. Transfer to a casserole dish.

Preheat oven to 150°C. ➤

Remove meat from marinade and set marinade aside. Pat meat dry, add to frying pan in batches and sauté until browned all over. Season with salt and freshly ground pepper. Transfer to casserole dish.

Pour a little of the marinade into the pan and stir to deglaze. Pour this into the casserole, adding reserved marinade and the tomatoes and orange zest. If liquid does not completely cover the meat, add a little water. Cover dish, place in preheated oven and cook for 3 hours. Check occasionally.

When meat is very tender, and coated in a thick sauce, stir through the tapenade.

Serve with creamy potato mash.

 Here this classic dish is given a twist – the salty tang of tapenade. Buy a good-quality tapenade, or make your own.

SERVES 6–8

Family beef & vegetable casserole

1 kg beef chuck steak, excess fat removed, cut into 2-cm squares

½ cup plain flour, seasoned with salt and pepper

1–2 tablespoons olive oil

2 cloves garlic, finely chopped

1 carrot, peeled and diced

1 parsnip, peeled and diced

2 teaspoons ground cardamom

2 teaspoons ground coriander

1 teaspoon ground allspice

1½ cups beef stock

creamy mash (page 194), to serve

Preheat oven to 160°C.

Dust beef with seasoned flour and brush off any excess. Heat 1 tablespoon of the oil in a large, non-stick frying pan over high heat. Cook beef in batches, turning, until browned all over. Transfer meat to a plate.

Reduce heat, add a little extra oil to pan if needed, then add vegetables and spices and cook, stirring, for about 1 minute or until fragrant. Pour in beef stock and stir. Bring to the boil, then remove from heat.

Transfer meat and sauce to a large casserole dish and cover. Place in preheated oven and bake for about 1½ hours, stirring occasionally, until beef is tender and sauce has thickened.

Serve with creamy mashed potato alongside.

SERVES 4

Florentine roast pork

4 cloves garlic, crushed

2 sprigs fresh rosemary, chopped

salt and freshly ground black pepper

1 kg boned loin of pork, rind removed

2 cloves

3 tablespoons olive oil

Mix garlic, rosemary, salt and pepper in a small bowl. Make several small slits in the pork and press a little of the garlic mixture into each slit. Rub the rest of the garlic mixture over the meat, press in the cloves, and drizzle with a tablespoon of the oil. Cover meat and place in refrigerator for several hours for flavours to develop.

Preheat oven to 180°C.

Put remainder of the oil in a roasting pan and add pork. Place in preheated oven and roast for 2 hours, turning and basting two or three times. For the last 10 minutes, increase the heat to 220°C to brown the meat surface.

When cooked, transfer meat to a plate, cover to keep warm and leave to rest for at least 10 minutes. **>**

Meanwhile, drain off fat from roasting pan. Add 3–4 tablespoons of water, place over a high heat and cook for a few minutes, stirring and scraping the pan to get all tasty residue and cooking juices, until it thickens to a gravy.

To serve, carve meat into slices and pour the gravy over.

 This roast pork is lovely hot with steamed spinach and roast potatoes, but also works well served cold with cannellini beans and a fresh green salad.

SERVES 6

Guinness veal with chat potatoes

6 pieces veal shank (osso buco)

3 tablespoons plain flour,
  seasoned with salt and pepper

2 tablespoons olive oil

1 clove garlic, crushed

2 onions, thickly sliced

2 cups Guinness stout

3 cups chicken or beef stock

2 bay leaves

2 tablespoons tomato paste

1 tablespoon caster sugar

salt and freshly ground pepper

12 steamed chat potatoes,
  to serve

Preheat oven to 180°C.

Dip veal pieces in the seasoned flour and dust off any excess.

Heat oil over medium heat in a flameproof casserole dish and sauté meat, in two batches, until browned all over. Transfer to a plate and set aside.

Lower heat, add garlic and onion to the dish and cook for 5–6 minutes, stirring occasionally, until softened. Increase heat, pour in the stout slowly, stir well and then boil gently for a few minutes until the liquid thickens and is reduced. Add stock, bay leaves, tomato paste and sugar, and stir well.

Return veal pieces to the pan. Cover, place in preheated oven and cook for 1½ hours, until the veal is tender.   **>**

Check dish for seasoning before serving with steamed chat potatoes.

 Stout might seem like an unusual pairing with veal, but it adds smoothness and complexity to the dish, without overpowering the other flavours. The sugar helps counteract any lingering acidity. You could substitute veal chops for the shank.

SERVES 4 – 6

Indian spice-crusted leg of lamb

2 tablespoons coriander seeds

2 tablespoons cumin seeds

1 tablespoon fenugreek seeds

2 teaspoons yellow mustard seeds

1 teaspoon dried chilli flakes

1 tablespoon ground turmeric

1 tablespoon ground cardamom

½ teaspoon ground ginger

2.5 kg butterflied lamb leg

½ cup olive oil

salt and freshly ground
    black pepper

Place coriander, cumin, fenugreek, mustard seeds and chilli flakes in a heavy-based frying pan over medium heat. Stir the spices and toast them until fragrant (about 1–2 minutes), but be careful not to let them burn. Cool, then place in a grinder (or use a mortar and pestle) and grind to a powder. Put the spices into a bowl, add the ground turmeric, cardamom and ginger, and stir to combine.

Place lamb in a dish and rub the spices in well. Cover with plastic wrap, refrigerate and leave to marinate for 5–6 hours, or overnight.

Preheat oven to 180°C.

Rub 3 tablespoons of the olive oil into the lamb and season with a little salt and a few twists of black pepper.

Place a large roasting pan over medium heat, add 1 tablespoon oil and, when it is hot, put in the lamb the lamb (fatty side down) and cook for **>**

about 5 minutes or until browned. Turn the lamb over and cook for a few more minutes until the other side is also browned.

Place lamb in preheated oven and roast for 35–40 minutes. If the crust is getting too dark, cover with aluminium foil. Transfer lamb to a serving plate or board, keep warm and rest for 10 minutes before carving into generous slices.

Serve with basmati rice, steamed spinach and a yoghurt and cucumber raita.

SERVES 8

Italian lamb ragu

4 tablespoons olive oil

1 red onion, chopped

3 cloves garlic, finely chopped

2 tablespoons chopped fresh
  rosemary

300 g stewing lamb, cut into
  small cubes

2 tablespoons tomato paste

200 ml red wine

400 g canned chopped tomatoes

½ cup good-quality black olives,
  pitted and sliced

salt and freshly ground
  black pepper

fettuccine or pappardelle,
  to serve

freshly grated parmesan cheese,
  and chopped flat-leaf parsley,
  to serve

Preheat oven to 120°C.

Heat oil in a flameproof casserole dish. Add onion, garlic and rosemary, and sauté for 5 minutes until onion has softened.

Increase heat and add lamb cubes in batches, sautéing until meat is browned all over. Stir in tomato paste and wine, and bring to the boil. Add the tomatoes, cover and simmer for 15 minutes, stirring occasionally.

Place dish in preheated oven and cook covered, for 3–4 hours. Check occasionally and add a little stock or water if the mixture is looking dry. ❯

When meat is very tender and sauce well reduced, stir in the olives, season with salt and pepper, and cook for a further 30 minutes.

Serve with fettuccine or pappardelle, sprinkled with parmesan cheese and chopped parsley.

SERVES 6−8

Lamb hot pot

1–2 tablespoons olive oil

1 kg lamb shoulder, cut into small cubes

1 clove garlic, chopped

1 onion, diced

1 carrot, peeled and diced

2 stalks celery, diced

1 tablespoon plain flour

750 ml beef stock

400 g canned chopped tomatoes

1 tablespoon tomato paste

1 tablespoon fresh thyme leaves

salt and freshly ground black pepper

1 kg potatoes, peeled and cut into rounds

2 tablespoons butter, melted

Preheat oven to 180°C.

Heat oil in a large, heavy-based frying pan and cook lamb in batches until golden-brown (add a little more oil if needed). Place lamb in casserole dish.

Heat a little extra oil in the pan, add garlic, onion, carrot and celery, and cook for about 5 minutes, stirring often, until vegetables are soft. Sprinkle plain flour over vegetables and stir in, then cook for 3–4 minutes, again stirring so it doesn't stick. Add stock, tomatoes, tomato paste and thyme, bring to the boil, reduce heat and simmer for 10 minutes. Check for seasoning and add salt and pepper if needed. **>**

Pour the prepared sauce over the lamb in the casserole dish. Arrange potato rounds on top of lamb, and brush with melted butter. Place casserole in preheated oven and cook, uncovered, for 2½ hours, brushing the potatoes with the casserole juices every half hour or so. When the dish is ready, the potatoes will be golden-brown on the surface and tender inside.

 You can use lamb chump chops instead of the cubed shoulder.

SERVES 4

Lamb shanks in an oriental braise

2 tablespoons plain flour

salt and freshly ground
black pepper

½ teaspoon Chinese
five-spice powder

4 lamb shanks,
French-trimmed

2 tablespoons peanut oil

1 onion, finely chopped

2 cloves garlic, crushed

1 small fresh red chilli,
deseeded, finely sliced

4 cups chicken stock

2 tablespoons red wine vinegar

3 tablespoons dark soy sauce

1 tablespoon medium-hot
chilli sauce

1 teaspoon hoisin sauce

2 star anise

1 cinnamon stick

creamy mash (page 194), to serve

Preheat oven to 180°C.

Mix together flour, salt, pepper and five-spice powder. Pat the lamb dry
then dust with the seasoned flour.

Heat oil in a flameproof casserole dish over medium heat. Add the shanks
and sauté for 6–7 minutes until brown all over, then transfer to a plate and
set aside. ➤

Add onion, garlic and chilli to the dish and cook, stirring, for a few minutes until the onion starts to soften. Add stock, vinegar, sauces and spices, and stir, then return the lamb to the casserole. Bring to the boil, cover, and place in preheated oven for 1½ hours. When it is cooked, the meat should be falling from the bone: remove dish from oven, transfer shanks to a plate and keep warm.

Strain the liquid into a small saucepan and cook over a high heat for several minutes until thickened and reduced.

To serve, put a layer of creamy mash on each plate, top with a lamb shank and pour the sauce over.

 French-trimmed (or 'Frenched') lamb shanks have the knuckle, skin and gristle removed from the ends. Most butchers sell the shanks prepared like this.

SERVES 4

Lamb shanks with tomato, white wine & white-bean mash

4 lamb shanks (about 350 g each), French-trimmed

3 tablespoons olive oil

1 brown onion, chopped

6 cloves garlic, peeled but left whole

fresh bouquet garni (see note page 25)

3 ripe tomatoes, peeled and quartered

4 semi-dried tomatoes, chopped

salt and freshly ground black pepper

¾ cup dry white wine

1¼ cups chicken or vegetable stock

800 g canned white beans

Heat oil in a heavy-based saucepan that will fit the lamb shanks in one layer. Fry shanks until brown all over. Transfer to a plate.

Add onion to the pan and cook, stirring, for 2–3 minutes, then add the garlic, bouquet garni, fresh and semi-dried tomatoes, and season with salt and pepper. Add the wine and stock, bring gently to the boil, cover, reduce the heat to very low and simmer for 1½ hours, until meat is falling from the bone. Check occasionally and add a little extra stock if needed.

Remove lid, and simmer for about 30 minutes to reduce and thicken sauce. Skim off any excess fat from the surface before serving.

To prepare the beans, rinse well, place in a saucepan with fresh water, bring to the boil and cook for 5 minutes until beans are heated. **>**

Drain and lightly crush (they should still have some texture, not be a purée). Season with salt and plenty of freshly ground pepper.

To serve, ladle a scoop of the warm crushed beans into each bowl and top with a lamb shank and some sauce.

 This dish improves in flavour if it is left overnight (refrigerated), in which case you can remove any fat that has set on the surface, before gently reheating. Instead of canned beans you can soak dried beans overnight and cook for 45 minutes until soft, then mash.

SERVES 4

Osso buco with gremolata

6 large pieces veal shank (osso buco), each about 2 cm thick

½ cup plain flour, seasoned with salt and pepper

5 tablespoons olive oil

1 medium-sized brown onion, finely chopped

2 medium-sized carrots, peeled and finely chopped

1 large stalk celery, finely chopped

1 bay leaf

1 cup dry white wine

2 cups veal or chicken stock

risotto (page 214) or creamy mash (page 194), to serve

gremolata (page 195)

Preheat oven to 160°C.

Trim rounded edges of the veal pieces so they do not curl while cooking, and tie the slices with kitchen string to hold them together. Dust meat with seasoned flour and shake off any excess.

Heat 3 tablespoons of the oil in a non-stick frying pan and sauté onion, carrots and celery for about 5 minutes, or until soft. Add bay leaf, then transfer vegetables to a casserole dish.

Add remaining oil to the pan and sauté the veal in batches until browned all over. Add wine and simmer until it has almost evaporated. Transfer meat to the casserole dish, standing pieces upright in a single layer, then pour stock over. Cover, place in preheated oven and cook for 2½ hours, **>**

until the meat is tender and falling off the bone (remove lid for the last half hour of cooking). If necessary, add a little more stock to the sauce to keep the meat moist.

To serve, place a veal piece on top of a bed of risotto or creamy mash, then sprinkle gremolata on top.

 The term *osso buco* (which means 'hollow bone') is used to describe both the cut of meat – a veal shank cut across the bone in 2–3-cm chunks – and the slow-cooked dish made with this cut, usually with wine and herbs and sometimes tomato. The bone marrow is what gives the dish its particularly rich flavour.

SERVES 4

Oxtail braise Moroccan-style

3 kg oxtail pieces, trimmed of fat

1 cup plain flour

1 tablespoon ground ginger

4 tablespoons olive oil

2 large onions, chopped

2 cloves garlic, finely chopped

3 stalks celery, chopped

1 teaspoon ground cinnamon

rind from 1 preserved lemon
 (page 211)

8 cloves

1 teaspoon ras al hanout
 (see note page 63)

800 g canned crushed tomatoes

2 bay leaves

zest of ½ orange

1½ cups red wine

2 cups beef or chicken stock

creamy mash (page 194), to serve

Preheat oven to 160°C.

Mix together the flour and ginger. Dredge oxtail in seasoned flour and dust off any excess.

Heat oil in a large, heavy-based flameproof casserole dish. Add meat in small batches and brown all over. Transfer to a dish and set aside.

Add onions, garlic, celery, cinnamon, preserved lemon, cloves and ras al hanout to the casserole and stir for a minute or so, until well mixed. Add tomatoes, bay leaves, orange zest and wine. Place browned oxtail in casserole dish, then add enough stock to cover the meat. **>**

Increase heat and bring to the boil. Cover dish, place in preheated oven and cook for 1 hour. Remove from oven, stir gently and cook for a further 1–1½ hours, until meat is falling from the bone and the sauce is brown and sticky.

Serve with the creamy mashed potatoes alongside.

SERVES 4

Oxtail stew

1 kg oxtail pieces, trimmed of fat

2 tablespoons plain flour, seasoned with salt and pepper

3 tablespoons olive oil

2 brown onions, chopped

2 cloves garlic, finely chopped

2 carrots, peeled and sliced

salt and freshly ground pepper

2 sprigs fresh thyme

1 bay leaf

400 g canned chopped tomatoes

2 cups beef or chicken stock

creamy mash (page 194), to serve

chopped parsley for garnish

Dredge the oxtail pieces in the seasoned flour, then dust off any excess.

Heat oil in a large, flameproof casserole dish over medium heat, then sauté the meat in batches until brown on all sides. Transfer meat to a plate.

Add onions, garlic and carrots to the casserole dish and sauté for 3–4 minutes until onion is just browning. Return oxtail pieces to the dish, and add salt and freshly ground pepper, thyme, bay leaf, tomatoes and stock. Stir well, bring liquid to the boil, then lower heat, cover with a tightly fitting lid, and simmer for 2½–3 hours. Check occasionally, stirring gently.

When meat is almost falling off the bones, transfer oxtail pieces to a heated dish and keep warm. Reheat the cooking liquid over medium to high heat, and as it heats keep skimming off any fat. The sauce will gradually thicken and reduce, and should be quite sticky.

To serve, place one or two oxtail pieces on a bed of mash, on individual plates, and spoon sauce over.

 This is definitely a dish that is even better the next day (or a few days later). If it is refrigerated overnight it is also easier to remove excess fat from the sauce, as the fat will set: you can refrigerate the meat and sauce separately, to make this easier.

SERVES 4–6

Pork belly with sage, pancetta & apples

6 tablespoons fennel seeds

2.5 kg boned pork belly

4 litres boiling water

3 whole heads garlic, unpeeled

12 thin slices pancetta

20 fresh sage leaves

sea salt and freshly ground
  black pepper

6 medium-sized onions, halved

6 bay leaves

2 tablespoons olive oil

8 small apples

2 cups water

½ cup white wine

1 cup chicken stock

Preheat oven to 150°C. Meanwhile, grind fennel seeds with a mortar and pestle, or in a spice grinder.

Place garlic heads in preheated oven and roast for 30 minutes. When cooked, push the flesh from the cloves into a bowl, and mash.

Increase oven temperature to 240°C.

Place pork, rind-side up, on an oven rack over a sink or draining board, and pour boiling water over to soften the skin. Place pork on a chopping board and, using a very sharp knife, score the skin with cuts about 2 cm apart (do not cut through to the meat). Rub roasted garlic pulp and half the ground fennel into the flesh. Lay pancetta slices over the seasoned meat, then scatter with the sage leaves and season with salt and freshly ground pepper.   **>**

Roll pork and tie securely with kitchen string every 4 cm or so. Mix remaining ground fennel with extra crushed salt and rub into the rind.

Lightly oil a large baking dish. Put onions and bay leaves on the base and place pork on top, rind-side up. Drizzle oil over, place dish in preheated oven and roast for 25–30 minutes, or until rind starts to crackle.

Score apples by peeling off a ring of skin (this stops them bursting) and add apples to roasting pan. Pour in 2 cups of water, reduce oven temperature to 150°C and roast for 1–1½ hours until skin is golden-brown and juices run clear when meat is pierced with a skewer.

Transfer cooked pork to a warmed platter, cover loosely and leave to rest for 15 minutes. Place onions and apples in another dish and keep warm. Remove as much fat as possible from pan, pour in wine and stir over high heat. Add stock and continue stirring until sauce thickens and reduces (this will take several minutes). Check for seasoning, and strain.

To serve, slice pork and serve with the apples, onions and sauce alongside.

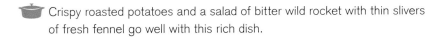 Crispy roasted potatoes and a salad of bitter wild rocket with thin slivers of fresh fennel go well with this rich dish.

SERVES 8

Pork roast & spiced peach chutney

2 kg boned pork loin

1 tablespoon olive oil

½ teaspoon caraway seeds

1 teaspoon sea salt

SPICED PEACH CHUTNEY

2 large ripe peaches, peeled and chopped

1 large brown onion, chopped

¼ cup sultanas

1 tablespoon grated fresh ginger

1 cup raw sugar

1 cup cider vinegar

1 cinnamon stick

2 cloves

Preheat oven to 220°C.

Remove rind from pork and set aside. Rub flesh with some of the oil, and sprinkle with the caraway seeds. Put pork on a wire rack in a large baking dish, place (uncovered) in preheated oven, and roast for 1 hour. To test if meat is cooked, pierce at thickest point with a skewer – if juices run clear, it is ready. Remove pork from oven, cover with aluminium foil and keep warm.

Raise oven temperature to 250°C.

To make crackling, cut away excess fat from underside of pork rind, use a very sharp knife to score the top, then rub with the rest of the oil and press on sea salt. Place rind, with the fatty side facing up, on wire rack in a baking dish. Place dish in oven and roast, uncovered, for about 15 minutes. Crackling is ready when crisp and brown. Drain on kitchen paper. ❯

To serve, slice pork and serve with crackling and peach chutney alongside.

To make the chutney, place all ingredients in a medium-sized saucepan and stir over medium heat until sugar is dissolved. Bring mixture to the boil, lower heat and simmer, uncovered, for about 1¾ hours, until chutney thickens.

 The peach chutney will keep (refrigerated) in a sterilised jar, for up to a week.

SERVES 6

Pot au feu

1.5 kg beef silverside or topside

1 kg beef (or veal) shank bones

3 litres beef stock or water

1 tablespoon salt

5 peppercorns

4 medium-sized carrots, peeled and cut into chunks

2 leeks, trimmed, rinsed, and cut into 6-cm lengths

2 medium-sized parsnips, peeled and cut into chunks

4 small waxy potatoes, peeled and cut into chunks

6 small pickling onions, peeled and each studded with a clove

fresh bouquet garni (see note page 25)

mustard, sour gherkins and good-quality sea salt, to serve

Place meat and bones in a large saucepan and cover with cold water. Bring to the boil, reduce heat to very low and simmer for 10 minutes. Drain off the liquid, leaving meat in the pot.

Add stock (or water), salt and peppercorns to the meat. Bring just to the boil and skim any fat or froth from the surface. Partially cover, and simmer on low heat for 2½ hours, occasionally skimming the surface. After this time, add carrots, leeks, parsnips, potatoes, onions and bouquet garni to the pot, then continue simmering very gently for a further hour. Continue to check the pot, skimming the surface. **>**

When meat is meltingly tender, remove bouquet garni and any bones, then transfer meat and vegetables to a warmed platter. Strain broth through a fine strainer and serve in soup bowls with crusty bread. Slice the meat and serve separately, with the vegetables and side dishes of mustard, gherkins and sea salt.

 This classic French one-dish meal – the name simply means 'pot on the fire' – is the epitome of slow cooking. Traditionally, the broth is served first, followed by the meat and vegetables.

SERVES 6

Red capsicums stuffed with beef & pine nuts

6 small to medium-sized red capsicums

chopped fresh basil, to serve

STUFFING

2 tablespoons olive oil

1 medium-sized onion, diced

250 g lean beef mince

90 g short-grain rice, rinsed

1 tomato, chopped

2 tablespoons chopped flat-leaf parsley

½ teaspoon ground allspice

½ teaspoon ras al hanout (see note page 63)

½ cup pine nuts, toasted

salt and freshly ground black pepper

SAUCE

1 red onion. diced

1 tablespoon olive oil

2 cups tomato passata (see note page 73)

2 tablespoons tomato paste

3–4 fresh basil leaves

Slice the stem end off each capsicum, and remove seeds and membranes.

To make stuffing, heat oil in a frying pan and sauté onion for a few minutes until soft. Add the beef mince and cook for 5 minutes, stirring occasionally, until lightly browned. Remove from heat and add rice, tomato, parsley, spices and pine nuts. Season with salt and freshly ground pepper.

Preheat oven to 180°C. ➤

To make the sauce, heat oil in a frying pan, sauté onion for 4–5 minutes or until soft, then add tomato passata and paste, and fresh basil leaves. Simmer for 5 minutes, then pour into a casserole dish large enough to hold the capsicums upright (they should fit together snugly).

Spoon stuffing into the capsicums (leave a little space at the top, as the rice will expand when it cooks), and place in the casserole dish on top of the tomato sauce. Cover, place in preheated oven and bake for 1 hour.

To serve, place one capsicum per person on each plate, spoon some sauce over and scatter with chopped basil.

SERVES 6

Rogan josh

3 tablespoons vegetable oil or ghee (clarified butter)

1.4 kg boneless lamb, cut into 2.5-cm cubes

2 teaspoons ground cardamom

2 teaspoons ground cumin

2 teaspoons ground coriander

1 teaspoon garam masala

2 brown onions, finely chopped

3 cloves garlic, crushed

2–3 fresh hot green chillies, deseeded and finely sliced

1 × 4-cm piece fresh ginger, grated

400 g canned crushed tomatoes

2 bay leaves

1 cinnamon stick

1 cup natural or Greek-style yoghurt

salt

steamed jasmine rice and fresh coriander leaves, to serve

Heat 2 tablespoons of the oil or ghee over medium to high heat in a large heavy-based saucepan. Cook lamb in batches until brown all over. Transfer to a plate.

Add remaining oil or ghee to the pan. Add spices and cook for 1–2 minutes until fragrance is released. Add onions, garlic, chillies and ginger, and cook, stirring, for 3–4 minutes until onion has softened. Return lamb to the pan, add tomatoes, bay leaves and cinnamon stick, and mix. Add 1 tablespoon of yoghurt and stir well, then gradually add the remainder a tablespoon at a time, stirring after each addition. Bring just to the boil, cover and simmer for 1¾ hours, until lamb is tender.

Remove lid, stir and cook for a further 10 minutes until sauce has reduced. Check for seasoning and add salt if necessary. Serve with steamed rice and a garnish of fresh coriander leaves.

 It's important to add the yoghurt a little at a time so that it doesn't separate or curdle. Creamy Greek-style yoghurt is the best variety for cooking.

SERVES 6

Shoulder of lamb
with lemon & saffron

3 tablespoons vegetable oil

1.1 kg boned lamb shoulder, cut into 10-cm pieces (ask your butcher to do this for you)

3 cloves garlic, finely chopped

3 onions, quartered

2 carrots, peeled and diced

2 stalks celery, chopped

juice of 1 lemon

grated zest of 2 lemons

2 tablespoons runny honey

2 pinches saffron threads

1 tablespoon plain flour

1.2 litres chicken stock

salt and freshly ground black pepper

steamed spinach, and creamy mash (page 194), to serve

Preheat oven to 150°C.

Heat 1 tablespoon of the oil in a flameproof casserole dish and sauté the lamb pieces in batches until well browned all over. Transfer to a plate and set aside.

Heat the remainder of the oil in the casserole, add garlic, onions, carrots and celery, and sauté for 4–5 minutes until softened. Return lamb to the casserole, add lemon juice and zest, honey and saffron, and sprinkle the flour over. Stir well and cook for 1 minute. Add stock and cook, stirring, until the liquid comes to the boil. Season to taste with salt and freshly ground pepper.   **>**

Cover dish, place in preheated oven and cook for 3–3½ hours, checking occasionally.

The lamb is ready when the sauce is thick and the meat is extremely tender. Season with salt and freshly ground pepper if needed.

Serve with steamed spinach and creamy mash.

SERVES 4

Slow-roasted Chinese pork belly with bok choy

2 kg pork belly, rind left on
3 tablespoons sea salt
½ cup hoisin sauce
2 tablespoons sugar
4 bunches bok choy, ends trimmed
steamed jasmine rice, to serve

Use a sharp knife to make slits in the pork rind, then rub in the salt. Rub hoisin sauce and sugar into the underside of the pork. Place meat in a clean dish, cover well and refrigerate overnight.

Preheat oven to 200°C.

Place pork in roasting dish and roast for 15 minutes. Lower heat to 180°C and roast for a further 2 hours. When meat is cooked, cover loosely to keep warm and leave for 10–15 minutes.

While meat is resting, rinse bok choy and, with water still clinging to the leaves, place in large saucepan, cover partially and cook for 5–6 minutes until just wilted.

Slice pork belly and serve with bok choy and steamed jasmine rice.

SERVES 8

Spezzatino di manzo

1 tablespoon unsalted butter

2 tablespoons olive oil

2 red onions, finely sliced

2 cloves garlic, crushed

about 20 fresh sage leaves

900 g stewing beef (e.g. blade or chuck), cut into 2.5-cm cubes

1 teaspoon ground paprika

1 cup robust red wine

1½ cups tomato passata (see note page 73)

1 teaspoon coarsely grated orange zest

salt and freshly ground black pepper

Melt the butter with the oil in a heavy-based saucepan over a medium heat. Sauté onion and garlic for 6–7 minutes until softened, add sage leaves and cook for a further minute.

Add beef in batches and sauté for about 8–10 minutes until well browned all over. Stir in paprika and wine, and boil, stirring, for a few minutes until wine is reduced by half. Sprinkle flour over the meat and cook for 1 minute until the sauce coats the meat. Add the tomato passata and orange zest, and season with salt and freshly ground pepper.

Bring sauce to the boil again, cover and simmer for 2 hours, until the meat is very tender. Check occasionally, and add a little hot water if meat or sauce is starting to stick.

SERVES 4–6

Spicy Italian sausages with cannellini beans

500 g dried cannellini beans
3 cloves garlic, peeled
salt and freshly ground black pepper
1 tablespoon fresh sage leaves
2 tablespoons olive oil
6 good-quality spicy Italian pork sausages (about 600 g total)
400 g canned chopped tomatoes
fresh Italian bread, to serve

Pick over beans to remove any impurities, cover well with cold water and soak overnight.

Drain beans, place in a saucepan with 2 whole garlic cloves and cover with plenty of cold water. Bring to the boil, remove any scum from the surface, then simmer for about 1–1½ hours until tender. Drain beans, and save a little of the cooking water.

Heat oil over a medium heat in a large heavy-based frying pan. Prick sausages with a fork and fry until well browned. Add one-third of the chopped garlic, plus the sage leaves, stir for about 1 minute and then add tomatoes. Simmer for 15 minutes, stirring once or twice, until tomatoes have cooked down to a sauce. **>**

Add the cooked and drained beans to the pot, stir well and check for seasoning, adding a little salt and pepper if necessary. Simmer for about 10 minutes, adding a little of the bean-cooking water if the mixture is too thick.

Serve with plenty of Italian bread to mop up the juices.

SERVES 6

Spicy lamb and red lentils

1 tablespoon vegetable oil

1 large onion, chopped

2 cloves garlic, crushed

200 g canned chopped tomatoes

300 g eggplant, cut in
small cubes

140 g red lentils, rinsed

300 g lean lamb, diced

1 teaspoon ground turmeric

2 teaspoons ground mild chilli

2 teaspoons ground cumin

1 teaspoon ground coriander

1 teaspoon muscovado or soft
brown sugar

1 tablespoon freshly squeezed
lemon juice

450 ml water

salt and freshly ground
black pepper

steamed rice, chopped fresh
coriander leaves, and plain
yoghurt, to serve

Heat oil in heavy-based, non-stick pan. Sauté onion and garlic, stirring, for about 5 minutes or until onion is soft. Add tomatoes, eggplant, lentils, lamb, turmeric, chilli, cumin, coriander, sugar, lemon juice and water. Bring to the boil, cover and simmer for 1 hour until tender.

Check seasoning, adding salt and pepper if needed. Remove from heat and stir through half the yoghurt and half the coriander.

Serve with steamed rice, a scoop of yoghurt and some chopped coriander.

SERVES 4

Spring navarin of lamb

1 kg boned lamb leg, cut into 5-cm chunks

4 tablespoons plain flour, seasoned with salt and pepper

2 tablespoons olive oil

2 cloves garlic, finely chopped

1 brown onion, cut into large chunks

4 medium-sized carrots, peeled and cut into 5-cm lengths

1 cup chicken stock

1 bay leaf

1 sprig fresh thyme

Dust the lamb pieces with the seasoned flour and brush off any excess.

Heat 2 tablespoons oil in a large flameproof casserole dish. Sauté the meat in batches, until brown all over, then transfer to a plate.

Add garlic, onion and carrots to the casserole dish and sauté for 2–3 minutes, stirring occasionally, until onion is softened and lightly brown. Return lamb to the casserole and season with salt and freshly ground pepper. Add stock, bay leaf and thyme. Bring to the boil, cover and simmer on low heat for 1 hour, or until meat is tender. Check and stir occasionally.

Transfer lamb to a warmed plate, cover and keep warm. Skim any excess fat from the top of the cooking juices, place the dish over a high heat and bring to the boil, stirring until the sauce thickens and reduces.

To serve, pour the sauce over the meat.

SERVES 4–5

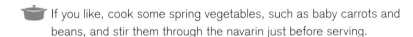 If you like, cook some spring vegetables, such as baby carrots and beans, and stir them through the navarin just before serving.

Steak & kidney pie

280 g ox kidney

600 g stewing beef, cut into 2.5-cm cubes

¾ cup plain flour, seasoned with salt and pepper

1 onion, diced

2 tablespoons chopped flat-leaf parsley

1 sprig fresh thyme

1 tablespoon tomato paste

1 tablespoon Worcestershire sauce

150 ml beef stock

1½ sheets ready-rolled puff pastry

1 egg, lightly beaten, for glazing

Preheat oven to 220°C.

Rinse kidney and well in cold water, pat dry then trim and finely slice.

Dust beef cubes and kidney slices with the seasoned flour and shake off any excess. Place meat, onion, parsley and thyme in a pie dish and lightly press down. Pour in the tomato paste, stock, and enough water to come halfway up the dish.

Cut one or two strips of pastry from the half sheet, to fit around the pie dish. Moisten the edge of the dish with water and press down the pastry strips. Brush pastry strips with water, then drape whole pastry sheet over, trim to fit and pinch edges to seal. Make a small hole in the centre for air to escape. Use pastry trimmings to decorate the lid. **>**

Place pie in refrigerator for 10 minutes to chill. Brush pastry with beaten egg, place pie in preheated oven and bake for 30 minutes. Reduce temperature to 180°C and bake for a further 90 minutes (if pastry is becoming too dark, cover with aluminium foil or baking paper).

 You can substitute lamb or veal kidneys for the ox kidney.

SERVES 4

Steak & mushroom pie

2 tablespoons olive oil

1 kg beef chuck steak, excess fat
   trimmed, cut into 4-cm cubes

1 large onion, chopped

2 cloves garlic, finely chopped

1 tablespoon plain flour,
   seasoned with salt and pepper

250 ml beef or chicken stock

400 g canned crushed tomatoes

250 g button mushrooms,
   trimmed and thickly sliced

2 sheets ready-rolled puff pastry

1 egg, lightly beaten, for glazing

Heat 1 tablespoon of oil in large, non-stick pan over medium–high heat. Sauté the beef in batches, turning until well browned. When cooked, transfer to a plate and set aside.

Add the rest of the oil to the pan over medium heat, then add onion and cook, stirring, until softened. Add garlic and cook for 1 minute. Sprinkle the flour over and cook, stirring, for another minute.

Add the stock and stir to mix in any residue from the base of the pan. Return beef to the pan and add crushed tomatoes. Cover and simmer over low heat, stirring occasionally, for 1 hour. Stir in the mushrooms and simmer, uncovered, for 45 minutes, until beef is tender and sauce has thickened.   **>**

Transfer the steak mixture to a 23-cm ovenproof pie dish. Leave to cool for 10 minutes, then cover with plastic wrap and refrigerate for 30 minutes until cold.

Preheat oven to 200°C.

Thaw the pastry if frozen. Cut strips 1.5-cm wide from one sheet, and press them around the edge of the pie dish. Cover the dish with the remaining pastry sheet and press edges together (trim off any overhanging pastry). Brush the beaten egg onto pastry to glaze. Make 3 or 4 small slits in the pastry, using a very sharp knife, place pie in preheated oven and bake for 25–30 minutes until pastry is golden.

SERVES 6

Tagine of lamb & quince

200 g dried chickpeas

2 tablespoons olive oil

1 kg lamb shoulder, cut into
cubes or chunks

2 cloves garlic, chopped

1 brown onion, finely chopped

1 teaspoon ground turmeric

1 teaspoon ground cumin

1 teaspoon ground ginger

1 teaspoon ground sweet paprika

pinch of saffron threads

1 cinnamon stick

2 quinces, peeled, cored
and quartered

2½ cups chicken stock

2 tablespoons honey

1 tablespoon freshly squeezed
lime juice

1 sweet potato, peeled and sliced

warmed flat bread, and couscous
(page 192), to serve

2 tablespoons chopped fresh
coriander leaves, to serve

Soak chickpeas in cold water overnight. Drain, place in a saucepan,
cover with fresh water and bring to the boil. Partially cover and simmer
for 45 minutes until tender, adding more water if necessary during
cooking time. Drain.

Heat oil in a large flameproof casserole dish over medium to high heat
and sauté lamb in batches until browned all over. Transfer to a plate and
set aside. ➤

Preheat oven to 170°C.

Add garlic and onion to casserole and cook until softened. Add ground spices, saffron threads and cinnamon stick, and cook for 1 minute, until fragrance is released. Return lamb to the casserole dish, add the quinces, stock, honey and lime juice, and bring to the boil. Cover dish, place in preheated oven and cook for 1½ hours, checking occasionally. After this time, add the cooked chickpeas and the sweet potato. Return to the oven for 30 minutes, until meat, quinces and sweet potato are very tender.

Serve with warmed flat bread, and couscous scattered with coriander leaves.

SERVES 4–6

 Prunes are often included in a tagine. Just add ½–¾ cup pitted prunes with the cooked chickpeas and the sweet potato.

Traditional shepherd's pie

1 tablespoon olive oil

1 brown onion, diced

1 clove garlic, crushed

1 medium-sized carrot, diced

2 stalks celery, finely chopped

500 g lean lamb mince

2 tablespoons plain flour

2 cups beef stock

1 bay leaf

1 tablespoon Worcestershire
sauce

1 tablespoon tomato paste

1 cup shelled peas, fresh
or frozen

salt and freshly ground
black pepper

200 g floury potatoes, peeled
and quartered

50 g butter

½ cup milk

melted butter, for glazing

Heat oil in a large non-stick pan over medium heat. Add onion, garlic, carrot and celery, and sauté, stirring, for 5 minutes. Add mince and continue stirring for about 7–8 minutes, or until lamb turns light brown. Add flour and cook for 2–3 minutes.

Add stock, bay leaf, Worcestershire sauce and tomato paste, and bring to the boil. Reduce heat, cover and simmer for 30 minutes, stirring occasionally, until sauce thickens. Stir the peas through, then test for seasoning. ➤

Meanwhile, cook potatoes in boiling water for 15 minutes, until soft. Drain, and while still warm add the butter and mash well. Stir the milk through until well mixed, then season with salt and freshly ground pepper.

Preheat oven to 180°C.

Spoon mince and vegetables into a wide, 2-litre ovenproof dish. Spread mashed potato over the top, make a pattern with a fork, then brush with melted butter.

Place in preheated oven and bake for 30 minutes until top is golden.

SERVES 4−6

Tuscan veal with fennel

1 tablespoon fennel seeds

3 tablespoons plain flour,
seasoned with salt and pepper

700 g lean veal, cubed

2 tablespoons olive oil

2 cloves garlic, finely chopped

½ fresh red chilli, deseeded
and finely chopped

½ cup dry white wine

2 large juicy tomatoes, peeled,
deseeded and chopped

salt and freshly ground
black pepper

1 small to medium-sized,
thinly sliced fennel bulbs

3 tablespoons finely chopped
flat-leaf parsley

extra small sprigs of parsley,
for garnish

Mix fennel seeds with the seasoned flour. Dust veal in flour and seed mix, shaking off any excess.

Heat oil in a heavy-based, non-stick frying pan. Add garlic and chilli, and sauté for 2–3 minutes until garlic is lightly browned. Add veal pieces in batches, and sauté until well browned. Pour in wine, add tomatoes and season to taste with salt and pepper. Bring to the boil, then simmer for about 50 minutes.

Add fennel slices, stir gently, and simmer for another 10 minutes. Stir the chopped parsley through just before serving, and garnish with the parsley.

SERVES 4–6

Veal chops braised in white wine

6-8 veal chops

2 tablespoons plain flour, seasoned with salt and pepper

3 tablespoons olive oil

3 cloves garlic, finely chopped

2 leeks, white part only, washed, thinly sliced

150 g field mushrooms, cleaned and sliced

1½ cups dry white wine

1 cup veal or chicken stock

1 bay leaf

extra salt and freshly ground black pepper

2 tablespoons chopped flat-leaf parsley, to serve

Preheat oven to 180°C.

Dust veal chops in seasoned flour, then shake off excess. Heat 1 tablespoon of the oil over medium heat in a non-stick frying pan and sauté garlic and leek for 6–7 minutes, or until soft and transparent. Add mushrooms and sauté for a few minutes, until mushrooms start to soften. Transfer to a casserole dish.

Add remaining 2 tablespoons of oil to the pan and fry chops in batches until golden, then transfer to casserole dish.

Pour white wine and stock into the pan and, over a medium heat, deglaze (stirring to remove any residue sticking to the base or sides of the pan), **>**

then pour sauce into casserole dish. Add bay leaves and season with salt and freshly ground pepper.

Cover, place in preheated oven and cook for 1 hour, checking occasionally and stirring gently. When cooked, the meat will be falling from the bone.

To serve, remove bay leaf and scatter dish with chopped parsley.

SERVES 6

Veal with olives & fetta mash

3 tablespoons olive oil

8 cloves garlic, peeled but left whole

150 g bacon, cut into strips

8 pieces (about 2 kg) veal shank (osso buco)

½ cup plain flour, seasoned with salt and pepper

1 cup dry white wine

400 g canned crushed tomatoes

1.5 litres chicken or stock

2 small sprigs fresh rosemary

200 g good-quality black olives

fetta mash (page 194) and gremolata (page 195), to serve

Preheat oven to 170°C.

Heat 2 tablespoons of the oil over medium heat in a large flameproof casserole dish. Add whole garlic cloves and bacon strips and cook, stirring, for 4 minutes or until garlic is lightly browned. Transfer to a plate with a slotted spoon.

Dust veal in seasoned flour, shake off excess, then sauté in batches over medium heat for 7–8 minutes or until golden-brown. Transfer to a plate.

Pour wine into casserole and simmer until reduced by half. Return veal to dish with tomatoes, stock and rosemary and bring to the boil. Cover, place in preheated oven and cook for 1½ hours or until tender. **>**

Add olives with the sautéed garlic and bacon, cover again and cook for a further 30 minutes.

Remove veal and vegetables from the sauce and set aside. Put casserole dish over a medium heat and cook, uncovered, stirring occasionally, for 30–35 minutes, until sauce is thickened and reduced. Return meat and vegetables to the dish and simmer for 10–15 minutes until they are reheated.

To serve, place a generous scoop of fetta mash on each plate, top with a piece of veal and sprinkle with gremolata.

SERVES 8

Vegetables & sides

Vegetables, like meat, can be transformed by slow cooking, releasing their juices but retaining all their goodness in the flavoursome sauces that pool around them.

When slow-roasted in the oven, vegetables such as tomatoes, capsicums and onions caramelise and reduce, and their flavour intensifies. Pulses and grains are the perfect foil for slow-cooked meats, soaking up the robust sauces and bold flavours, but can also make a super-satisfying meal on their own.

If 'slow food' incorporates the notion of sourcing local and seasonal produce, this is especially the case with fresh vegetables. So take the time to search out locally grown ingredients whenever possible.

< Braised fennel (page 190)

Braised fennel

6 small bulbs fennel
2 tablespoons olive oil
freshly ground black pepper
1 cup chicken stock

Preheat oven to 160°C.

Trim the fennel bulbs, removing the core at the base and reserving some of the feathery fronds for garnish. Cut each bulb in half lengthways.

Heat olive oil in a flameproof casserole dish and sauté fennel pieces until golden on both sides. Season with freshly ground pepper and pour the stock over. Cover tightly, place in preheated oven and bake for 1 hour.

To serve, sprinkle with finely chopped fennel fronds.

SERVES 6

Caramelised baked onions

6 large onions

1 tablespoon brown sugar

1 tablespoon chopped fresh thyme leaves

salt and freshly ground black pepper

3 tablespoons balsamic vinegar

3 tablespoons olive oil

8 tablespoons water (may need extra during cooking)

Preheat oven to 200°C.

Cut onions in half crossways and place them, cut side down, in a roasting pan or ovenproof dish just large enough to hold them in one layer. Sprinkle with the sugar and herbs, and season with salt and freshly ground pepper. Pour balsamic, oil and water over onions.

Cover dish with a lid or aluminium foil, then place in preheated oven and bake for 20 minutes. Uncover, baste with the juices and bake for another 40 minutes (add a little extra water if necessary). The onions are cooked when tender and with a sticky brown coating.

SERVES 6

Couscous

2 cups couscous

salt

2 cups boiling water or stock

4 teaspoons butter or olive oil

Place couscous and salt in a small bowl. Pour boiling water (or stock) over and cover bowl with plastic wrap. Leave in a warm place for 5 minutes to allow the grains to expand.

Add butter and fluff with a fork to separate grains.

VARIATIONS

Nut & berry couscous: Toast slivered almonds and stir through couscous before serving. Alternatively, add pistachio nuts and cranberries or barberries.

Herbed couscous: When adding the butter, stir through 1 tablespoon each of chopped fresh flat-leaf parsley and mint, and sprinkle with 50 g flaked and toasted almonds.

SERVES 4

Creamy mash

1.2 kg floury potatoes, peeled and quartered
100 g butter
½ cup milk
salt and freshly ground pepper

Place potatoes in cold water in a medium-sized saucepan, bring to the boil and cook for 15–20 minutes, or until tender. Drain, mash with butter while still warm, then mix in milk. Add salt and freshly ground pepper to taste.

VARIATIONS

Horseradish mash: Omit pepper, and mix 2 tablespoons of prepared horseradish through the mashed potatoes.

Fetta mash: Omit butter, crumble 50 g of fetta and mix well into the mashed potatoes.

Mustard mash: Omit pepper and stir 2 tablespoons seeded French mustard through the mashed potatoes.

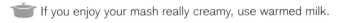 If you enjoy your mash really creamy, use warmed milk.

SERVES 4

Gremolata

zest of 1 lemon, finely chopped

½ cup finely chopped flat-leaf parsley

1 clove garlic, finely chopped

1 salted anchovy fillet, rinsed and finely chopped (optional)

freshly ground black pepper

Mix all the ingredients together in a bowl and set aside until ready to use.

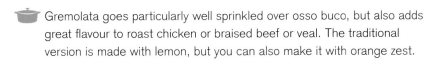 Gremolata goes particularly well sprinkled over osso buco, but also adds great flavour to roast chicken or braised beef or veal. The traditional version is made with lemon, but you can also make it with orange zest.

MAKES ½ CUP

Leeks braised in red wine

80 g butter

6 medium-sized leeks, white part only

salt and freshly ground black pepper

2 tablespoons plain flour

2 cups red wine (such as a shiraz)

2 cloves garlic

fresh bouquet garni (see note page 25)

Cut leeks in half and wash well to remove any grit.

Melt butter over low heat in a flameproof casserole dish. Place leeks in the casserole and season with salt and freshly ground pepper. Turn leeks until they are coated with the butter, then cook over medium heat for 4–5 minutes, stirring occasionally.

Sprinkle flour into the dish and toss to coat leeks. Pour in wine, add garlic and bouquet garni, cover tightly and simmer over a very low heat for 1 hour.

Remove bouquet garni before serving the leeks.

SERVES 6

Lemon & coriander pilaf

2 tablespoons unsalted butter

1 small onion, finely chopped

2 cups basmati rice, rinsed and drained

grated zest of ½ lemon

juice of 1 lemon

1 teaspoon crushed coriander seeds

3 cups water

1 cup milk

2 teaspoons sea salt

2–3 tablespoons chopped fresh coriander leaves

Melt butter in a medium-sized saucepan over medium heat. Add onion and cook for 3–5 minutes, stirring occasionally, until softened. Add the rice and stir until coated, then add the lemon zest, juice and coriander seeds. Add water and bring to the boil. Pour in milk, add salt, stir and bring back to the boil. Reduce heat, cover and simmer for 15 minutes.

Remove from heat, keep covered and leave to sit for 5 minutes.

To serve, fluff rice with a fork and sprinkle with fresh coriander leaves.

SERVES 6

Lima beans with rosemary & tomato

500 g dried lima beans
1 tablespoon olive oil
2 cloves garlic, crushed
1 medium-sized onion, finely chopped
3 tablespoons chopped flat-leaf parsley
1 tablespoon chopped fresh rosemary
400 g canned crushed tomatoes
salt and freshly ground black pepper

Place beans in a large bowl, cover with plenty of water and soak overnight or for 8 hours. Drain.

Put beans in a saucepan, cover with fresh water and bring to the boil. Boil for 10 minutes, skim the surface, then reduce heat, cover and simmer for 1 hour, checking occasionally. When soft, drain and set aside.

Heat oil over medium heat in a large non-stick saucepan. Add garlic and onion, and sauté, stirring, for 5 minutes or until onion is soft. Add parsley, rosemary and tomatoes and bring to the boil. Reduce heat, cover and simmer for 20–25 minutes, until sauce thickens. Add cooked and drained beans, season to taste and simmer for another 15 minutes.

SERVES 6

Middle Eastern eggplant & lentil stew

1 large eggplant (approx. 675 g)

100 g brown lentils

1 onion, finely chopped

4 cloves garlic, crushed

2 tomatoes, peeled and chopped

2 green chillies, seeded and chopped

2 tablespoons chopped fresh mint leaves

1 tablespoon tomato paste

1 teaspoon ras al hanout (see note page 63)

1 teaspoon salt

freshly ground black pepper

½ cup olive oil

3 tablespoons pomegranate molasses (see note page 81)

plain yoghurt and extra fresh mint leaves, to serve

Cut eggplant in half lengthways and then cut across into slices about 2 cm thick.

Place lentils in a small saucepan, cover with water and bring to the boil. Skim the surface of any scum, reduce heat and simmer for about 15 minutes, or until tender. Drain.

Place onion, garlic, tomatoes, chilli, mint leaves, tomato paste, ras al hanout, salt and pepper in a bowl and toss to mix.

Brush the inside of a heavy-based, flameproof casserole dish with 1 tablespoon of the oil. Spoon some of the onion mix into the casserole, **>**

top with half the eggplant slices, then half the lentils. Repeat layers, top with the remainder of the oil and drizzle pomegranate molasses over.

Place casserole over medium to high heat and bring to the boil. Reduce heat to very low, cover and simmer for about 1½ hours, until eggplant is completely tender.

When cooked, sprinkle with mint leaves and serve with a bowl of yoghurt on the side.

SERVES 4

Mujadarra (lentils and rice)

½ cup olive oil

1 brown onion, finely chopped

1 cup green lentils, rinsed

3¾ cups water

½ teaspoon ground allspice

1 cinnamon stick

2 teaspoons salt

freshly ground black pepper

1 cup basmati rice, rinsed

Heat oil in a frying pan over medium heat and sauté onion for 3–5 minutes or until soft and lightly browned. Add lentils, water, allspice and cinnamon, then bring to the boil. Reduce heat, partially cover and simmer for 20 minutes or until tender.

Add the salt and plenty of freshly ground pepper, then stir in rice. Bring to the boil again, reduce to lowest heat, cover and simmer for a further 20 minutes.

Remove cinnamon stick before serving.

 This can be served as a main course with finely sliced, caramelised onion rings and a scoop of yoghurt on top, but also works well as a side dish.

SERVES 5–6

Oven-baked beetroot with yoghurt

12 small beetroot
3 tablespoons olive oil
salt and freshly ground pepper
1 cup Greek-style yoghurt
fresh mint leaves, to serve

Preheat oven to 180°C.

Scrub beetroot well (wear rubber gloves to avoid standing your hands).
Trim the stalk end, but leave the feathery tail intact. Place them in a baking
tray, pour over the oil and toss them to make sure they are coated. Bake in
preheated oven for about 1 hour, or until tender.

To serve, cut into thick slices and serve with yoghurt and fresh mint leaves.

 This serves 4 as a side dish, but you can use larger beetroot and serve
with couscous and a salad for a light meal.

SERVES 4

Polenta, char-grilled

olive oil, for oiling pan and grilling

3 cups water

1 cup chicken or vegetable stock

1 teaspoon salt

250 g polenta

salt and freshly ground black pepper

Lightly oil a 20-cm × 30-cm lamington pan.

Place water, stock and salt in a large saucepan and bring to the boil. Pour in the polenta in a slow, steady stream, stirring constantly. Reduce heat to low and simmer, stirring occasionally, for 10 minutes, until polenta is thick (keep stirring and scraping down the sides of the pan). Season with salt and freshly ground pepper.

Pour polenta into oiled lamington pan, smooth the surface. Cover with cling wrap and leave to cool. When set, cut into serving portions, brush lightly on both sides with oil and grill under a very hot grill, or on a grill pan, for about 2–3 minutes each side, until hot and slightly charred.

SERVES 4 AS A SIDE DISH

Polenta, soft

4 cups water or stock
1 teaspoon salt
250 g polenta
1 cup milk
½ cup freshly grated parmesan cheese
60 g butter
salt and freshly ground black pepper

Place water and salt in a large saucepan and bring to the boil. Pour in polenta in a slow, steady stream, stirring constantly. Reduce heat to low and simmer, stirring occasionally, for 10 minutes, until polenta is thick. Add milk, stir well and simmer for a further 10 minutes. You need to keep stirring and scraping down the sides of the pan.

Remove pan from the heat, add parmesan cheese and butter, and stir. Season with salt and freshly ground pepper.

 Soft polenta is similar in texture to creamy mashed potato, and it is an excellent base for slow-cooked meat and vegetables, soaking up the flavour-rich sauces.

SERVES 4–6

Potatoes boulangère

1 kg floury potatoes
60 g unsalted butter
255 g onions, thinly sliced
1 sprig fresh rosemary or thyme
1 bay leaf

1 clove garlic, crushed
2 tablespoons finely chopped,
  fresh flat-leaf parsley
1.5 litres hot chicken stock
freshly ground pepper

Preheat oven to 190°C.

Peel potatoes, cut into very thin slices and place in a bowl of cold water (to stop them going brown). Meanwhile, melt half the butter in a non-stick frying pan, add onions, rosemary or thyme, bay leaf and garlic, and sauté for 4–5 minutes until softened. Add parsley, stir and then remove from heat.

Drain potatoes and pat dry on kitchen paper. In a shallow baking dish layer potatoes and onions, finishing with a layer of potatoes. Pour the chicken stock gently over, dot with the remaining butter and add a few twists of pepper. Place in preheated oven and bake for 1 hour. The potatoes should be crispy on top but soft and tender underneath (pierce with a skewer to check).

SERVES 4

Preserved lemons

12 lemons (thin-skinned)

350 g sea salt

1 tablespoon crushed coriander seeds

2 cinnamon sticks

6 black peppercorns

2 bay leaves

1 cup freshly squeezed lemon juice

3 cups warm water

Wash and dry lemons. Cut lengthways into quarters, leaving them joined at the base. Put a heaped teaspoon of salt into the middle of each lemon and close up. Arrange in a sterilised 2-litre jar, sprinkling each layer with more salt. Add coriander, cinnamon, peppercorns and bay leaves.

Pour lemon juice and warm water into jar until lemons are covered. Place jar in a cool, dry place for at least a month before using. To use, rinse the lemons, discard the flesh and use only the rind.

 Preserved lemons add extra tang to oxtail stews, baked lamb or chicken, or can be added to risottos or pilafs.

Red cabbage braised with apple & balsamic

2 tablespoons butter

2 tablespoons olive oil

2 medium-sized red onions, thinly sliced

750 g red cabbage, finely shredded

2 large golden delicious apples, peeled, cored and cubed

½ cup raisins

1 bay leaf

1 tablespoon brown sugar

salt and freshly ground black pepper

1 cup balsamic vinegar

Heat butter and oil in a large flameproof casserole over medium heat. Add onion slices and sauté for 1–2 minutes, then add 2 tablespoons water, cover and simmer for 8–10 minutes, until onions have softened.

Add shredded cabbage, apple and raisins, and stir. Add bay leaf, sugar, salt, pepper and balsamic and stir again gently. Cover and simmer over low heat for 2½ hours, checking occasionally. Add some extra water during the cooking time if the mixture is getting too dry.

When cooked, transfer to a dish and cover until cool, then refrigerate.

 This braise improves in flavour, so is best prepared at least a day in advance. Reheat before serving (it's especially good with spicy sausages, slow-cooked veal, and pork).

SERVES 4

Risotto milanese

pinch of saffron threads

3½ cups hot chicken stock

¼ cup olive oil

1 medium-sized onion, finely chopped

2 cups arborio or carnaroli rice

½ cup white wine

3 tablespoons butter

½ cup freshly grated parmesan cheese

freshly ground black pepper

extra grated parmesan, to serve

Add the saffron threads to the chicken stock, stir well and leave to infuse for at least 15 minutes.

Heat oil in a medium-sized saucepan over medium heat. Add onion and sauté for 5–6 minutes until soft but not browned. When onion is ready, add rice and stir for 2–3 minutes until it is well coated with oil. Add wine and cook for another minute until it is absorbed. Add one or two ladlefuls of stock at a time, stirring after each addition, until the liquid is absorbed.

Keep adding stock, a little more each time. After about 15 minutes, you should have used all the stock and the rice should be creamy but al dente (cooked but with a little 'bite').

Add butter, cheese and some freshly ground black pepper and stir well. Serve immediately, with a little extra parmesan cheese sprinkled on top.

 Risotto is delicious on its own, but it also makes a perfect accompaniment to slow-cooked meat dishes. Although it doesn't take very long to cook (around 20 minutes), to make it in the traditional way you do have to keep stirring for most of that time. This recipe is for a classic risotto milanese, subtly flavoured and coloured with saffron, with just enough of its own flavour to be an excellent foil to other dishes.

SERVES 6–8 AS A SIDE DISH

Rosemary potatoes

6 large potatoes (desirée or pink-eye are good)
1–2 tablespoons fruity olive oil
sea salt and freshly ground black pepper
2 sprigs fresh rosemary

Preheat oven to 180°C.

Scrub potatoes well and then pat dry. Cut several deep slits in the top of each potato, but do not cut through.

Place potatoes in a baking dish, add oil, salt and pepper, and toss until potatoes are coated. Add sprigs of rosemary, then place in preheated oven and bake for 1 hour. Turn potatoes over, increase oven temperature to 200°C and bake for a further 15 minutes, until potatoes are crisp and brown on the outside.

SERVES 6

Salsa verde

1 cup firmly packed fresh flat-leaf parsley leaves

2 cloves garlic, crushed

1 tablespoon drained capers

4 anchovy fillets, drained

1 teaspoon grated lemon zest

⅓ cup extra-virgin olive oil

salt and freshly ground black pepper

Place first five ingredients in a blender and whizz until combined. Gradually add oil until a chunky paste forms. Taste, and season if desired (the anchovies and capers make it quite salty).

Cover with plastic wrap until ready to use. Salsa verde will keep, well covered in the refrigerator, for 2–3 days and improves as the flavours develop.

SERVES 6

Skordalia

300 g floury potatoes, peeled and cut into quarters
6 large cloves garlic, crushed
⅔ cup extra-virgin olive oil
1 tablespoon freshly squeezed lemon juice
1 egg yolk
salt and freshly ground black pepper

Place potatoes in a medium-sized saucepan with cold water, bring to the boil and cook for 10–15 minutes or until soft. Drain well.

Meanwhile, mix olive oil, lemon juice and egg yolk and whisk lightly.

When potatoes are cooked, drain and place in a bowl. Add garlic, salt and pepper, and use an electric mixer to beat for 6–7 minutes until smooth. With mixer still going, slowly pour in oil mixture and beat until creamy.

 This pungent, garlic-laced potato mash is a Greek classic, ideal to soak up the sauce from slow-cooked meats, especially traditional lamb dishes.

MAKES ABOUT 1 CUP

Slow-roasted balsamic tomatoes

8 good-quality ripe tomatoes

2 tablespoons olive oil

4 tablespoons balsamic vinegar

4 tablespoons brown sugar

3 tablespoons fresh thyme leaves

Preheat oven to 120°C.

Slice tomatoes in half and place, cut-side down, in an ovenproof dish.
Mix oil, vinegar and brown sugar, then sprinkle over tomatoes and scatter
with thyme leaves. Place in preheated oven and roast for 1–1½ hours.

 These can be served hot with a roast, with grilled chicken, meat or soft
polenta (page 208), or at room temperature topped with a small scoop
of olive tapenade and served with crusty bread as a starter. They will
keep, well covered, in the refrigerator for several days.

SERVES 8 AS A STARTER OR SIDE DISH

Sweets

The aroma of apples baking, the heady scent of cinnamon from a creamy custard, and the unbeatable fragrance of a chocolate cake fresh from the oven — all these are the result of slow cooking.

It can take a little extra time to prepare and cook these special treats, but the rewards are rich.

< Baked lime delicious pudding (page 224)

Baked lime delicious pudding

2 eggs, separated
40 g butter
225 g caster sugar
2 tablespoons self-raising flour, sifted
juice and grated zest of 2 limes
1 cup milk
icing sugar and double cream, to serve

Preheat oven to 150°C.

Beat egg yolks until well mixed. In a separate bowl, beat egg whites until stiff.

Cream butter and sugar until pale. Fold in flour, lime juice and zest, milk and egg yolks. When well mixed, fold in beaten egg whites.

Pour mixture into an ovenproof pie dish, set this in a baking dish and add enough boiling water to come halfway up the sides of pie dish. Place in preheated oven and bake for 45–60 minutes, until set and golden on top.

Serve dusted with icing sugar and sprinkled with shredded lime zest if you like, with cream on the side.

SERVES 4

Chocolate cake
with chocolate ganache

200 g self-raising flour

25 g Dutch cocoa powder

250 g brown sugar

125 g butter, softened

2 eggs

1 teaspoon vanilla extract

2 teaspoons brandy

150 ml water

CHOCOLATE GANACHE

160 ml thick cream

160 g good-quality dark
chocolate, chopped

½ teaspoon unsalted butter

Preheat oven to 170°C. Grease a 20-cm round cake pan and line with non-stick baking paper.

Sift flour and cocoa into a medium-sized bowl. Add sugar, butter, eggs, vanilla, brandy and water. Beat on low speed with electric mixer until ingredients are combined, then increase speed and beat for 3–4 minutes until mixture is smooth and light. Pour batter into prepared cake pan and place in preheated oven. Bake for 50–55 minutes, or until a skewer inserted in the centre of the cake comes out clean.

Leave cake to cool for 5 minutes in the pan before inverting onto a cooling rack. ➤

Meanwhile, make the ganache: pour cream into a small saucepan and bring slowly to the boil, then remove from heat, add chocolate and beat until chocolate is melted. Whisk in butter, then leave to cool a little.

When cake is almost cool, pour the ganache over. (You might like to place a sheet of baking paper under the cooling rack to catch any drips.) The ganache layer should not be too thick – if it is, add a little more cream. Leave to set before serving.

 If you don't need all the ganache, you can refrigerate it and gently reheat to serve as a luscious sauce with ice-cream.

SERVES 8–10

Chocolate jaffa self-saucing pudding

2 eggs, at room temperature

finely grated zest of 1 orange

110 g caster sugar

100 g self-raising flour

1 tablespoon Dutch cocoa
powder

1 tablespoon hot water

2 teaspoons melted butter

2 teaspoons orange liqueur

icing sugar and cream, or
ice-cream, to serve

SAUCE

1¼ cups boiling water

100 g brown sugar

2 tablespoons Dutch cocoa
powder, sifted

Preheat oven to 180°C. Lightly grease a 4-cup ovenproof baking dish.

Place eggs and orange zest in a medium-sized bowl and whisk with electric beater until light and frothy. Gradually beat in caster sugar and whisk for 1–2 minutes, until mixture is thick.

Sift together flour and cocoa powder, and fold gently into the egg mixture. When it is almost incorporated, add water, melted butter and orange liqueur and stir until just mixed. Pour batter into prepared baking dish.

To make sauce, mix boiling water, sugar and cocoa in a bowl. Pour the sauce slowly over the back of a metal spoon over the pudding batter.

Place dish in preheated oven and bake for 45 minutes (the pudding is cooked when firm to the touch in the centre). Leave pudding to stand for 10 minutes before serving.

Serve lightly dusted with icing sugar, with thick cream or vanilla ice-cream.

SERVES 4–6

Golden polenta & olive oil cake

175 g self-raising flour, sifted

1 teaspoon baking powder

225 g caster sugar

50 g coarse polenta

225 ml light olive oil

4 eggs (60 g size)

juice and finely grated zest
of 1 small orange

juice and finely grated zest
of 1 lemon

icing sugar, to serve (optional)

Preheat oven to 170°C. Grease a 20-cm round cake tin and line with baking paper.

Place flour, baking powder, sugar and polenta in a bowl and mix. Make a well in the centre and pour in the oil. Drop in eggs one at a time, mixing with a wooden spoon to make a smooth, thick batter.

Lightly beat in the orange and lemon juice and zest. Spoon mixture into prepared tin and smooth surface. Place in preheated oven and bake for 1–1¼ hours. Cake is ready when firm to touch and starting to shrink from sides of tin. (If top is getting too dark during baking, cover with aluminium foil.) Leave cake to cool for 10 minutes before transferring to a cooler.

If desired, dust lightly with icing sugar before serving.

SERVES 8

Jane's baked nutmeg custard

4 cups (1 litre) pouring cream
1 vanilla bean
4 eggs (60 g size)
220 g caster sugar
½ teaspoon ground nutmeg
freshly grated nutmeg, to serve

Preheat oven to 150°C. Lightly grease a 30-cm × 22-cm ovenproof baking dish.

Place cream in a saucepan. Split the vanilla bean and scrape seeds into pan, then drop in the pod. Heat cream until it just comes to the boil, remove vanilla pod and leave cream to cool while you mix the eggs.

Place eggs and sugar in a bowl and beat well. Pour cream into egg mixture, and whisk to combine. Strain slowly into prepared dish, and sprinkle ground nutmeg over the top. Stand dish in a baking pan and pour in hot water to come halfway up the sides of the dish. Place in preheated oven and bake for 1 hour, or until custard is set (it should still have a slight wobble). Leave it to sit for a few minutes after removing from oven.

To serve, sprinkle with freshly grated nutmeg.

SERVES 6

Old-fashioned golden-syrup pudding

190 g self-raising flour, sifted

1 teaspoon baking powder

½ teaspoon mixed spice

150 g butter, softened

3 eggs, at room temperature

150 g caster sugar

4 tablespoons golden syrup

custard and freshly grated cinnamon, to serve

Lightly grease a 1.5-litre metal pudding basin with a lid. Cut a circle of baking paper to fit inside the top of the basin and butter it on one side.

Mix flour, baking powder and mixed spice in a medium-sized bowl. Add butter, eggs, sugar and 2 tablespoons of the golden syrup. Beat with an electric mixer on low speed until blended, then beat on medium speed for about 2 minutes or until smooth and lighter in colour.

Put the remaining 2 tablespoons of golden syrup in bottom of pudding basin, then spoon in batter mixture. Smooth surface with the back of the spoon, then cover with greased paper. Clip on the lid.

Place a trivet or saucer in the base of a deep saucepan, then place the basin on it. Add enough boiling water to reach two-thirds of the way up **>**

the sides of the basin. Cover saucepan, bring water to the boil over a medium heat, then reduce heat to a simmer and steam pudding for 2 hours. To keep the lid on firmly, you may need to weight it using cans of food.

Check the saucepan while the pudding is steaming to make sure it stays simmering (not boiling, or off the boil). Try not to lift the lid too often or the pudding will not steam at an even temperature and will not be light and fluffy. After 1 hour, lift the lid and top up to the original level, using boiling water.

To check if pudding is cooked, remove basin carefully from saucepan, remove lid (take care of steam) and insert a skewer. If the skewer comes out clean, the pudding is cooked.

Allow the pudding to stand for 5 minutes before inverting onto a warmed serving plate. Leave it for 1–2 minutes before cutting.

Serve with custard and dusted with freshly grated cinnamon.

 Placing the pudding basin on a trivet or saucer stops it touching the bottom of the saucepan, which can make the bottom of the pudding burn.

SERVES 6

Oven-roasted quinces with star anise

1.5 litres water

135 g caster sugar

2.5 kg quinces

1 strip lemon zest

1 cinnamon stick

2 cardamom pods

1 star anise

180 ml freshly squeezed lemon juice

crème fraîche or double cream, to serve (optional)

Preheat oven to 180°C.

Put water and sugar in a saucepan. Place over medium heat and stir until dissolved, but without boiling.

Wash quinces well, but do not peel. Place in a large ovenproof dish, add zest and spices, and pour sugar syrup over. Cover with a lid or aluminium foil. Place in preheated oven and roast for about 3½ hours, turning every hour or so. The fruit is ready when soft and deep pink in colour.

Remove from oven and leave to cool, then peel quinces.

Serve warm or at room temperature, alone or with crème fraîche or cream.

SERVES 6

Pecan & cranberry bread-and-butter pudding

100 g pecans

8 slices firm white bread, crusts removed

50 g butter, melted

½ cup dried cranberries

4 eggs

150 g caster sugar

375 ml cream

500 ml milk

1 teaspoon vanilla extract

vanilla ice-cream or yoghurt, to serve

Place pecans under grill and toast lightly for 1–2 minutes (watch closely – they will burn quickly). Chop roughly.

Cut bread slices in half and brush with melted butter. Lay slices, overlapping, in a shallow ovenproof dish, sprinkling with cranberries and pecans between layers.

Whisk eggs, sugar, cream, milk and vanilla together. Pour over bread and leave to stand for 15 minutes.

Preheat oven to 180°C. ➤

Stand ovenproof dish in a large baking pan and add enough boiling water to come halfway up the side. Place in preheated oven and bake, uncovered, for about 50 minutes until custard sets. If top is getting too brown, cover with baking paper or aluminium foil until the pudding is ready.

Serve hot or cold, with vanilla ice-cream or yoghurt.

SERVES 8

Roasted pears with mascarpone

8 beurre bosc pears

160 ml sauterne-style dessert wine

3 tablespoons olive oil

4 tablespoons caster sugar

1 tablespoon water

250 g mascarpone, to serve

Preheat oven to 180°C.

Peel pears, cut in half and remove core but leave stem attached. Place pears in an ovenproof baking dish, pour wine, oil and water over, and sprinkle with the sugar. Place in preheated oven and roast for 45–50 minutes, turning occasionally and basting with the syrupy juices.

When pears are soft and syrup has caramelised, remove from oven and leave for a few minutes. Serve just warm, drizzled with syrup and a scoop of mascarpone.

SERVES 8

Scottish dundee cake

100 g raisins

100 g currants

80 g sultanas

60 g glacé cherries

60 g mixed peel

grated zest of 1 orange

grated zestof 1 lemon

2 tablespoons whisky

170 g plain flour

1 teaspoon baking powder

1 teaspoon mixed spice

170 g unsalted butter, softened

170 g caster sugar

4 eggs

60 g almond meal

80 g blanched almonds

Place dried fruit and peel in a bowl with the grated orange and lemon zest and the whisky. Cover and set aside for 1 hour.

Preheat oven to 150°C. Grease base and sides of a non-stick 20-cm springform cake pan and line with baking paper.

Sift flour, baking powder and mixed spice together.

Place butter and sugar in a bowl and beat with an electric mixer until creamy. Add eggs one at a time and beat after each addition. Gently fold in sifted flour mixture and almond meal until well combined. Stir in the whisky-soaked fruits.

Pour batter into prepared pan, place in preheated oven and bake for
1¼ hours.

Remove cake from oven and arrange blanched almonds in a pattern on top.
Return cake to oven and bake for a further 1 hour. (If cake is getting too
brown, cover with baking paper or aluminium foil until it is cooked.) The cake
is cooked when a skewer inserted in the middle comes out clean. Cool well
before removing from the cake pan and transferring to a cake rack.

SERVES 6–8

Slow-roasted summer fruits with crème fraîche

80 g butter

¾ cup brown sugar

3 tablespoons water

1 vanilla bean, split in half lengthways

3 medium-sized peaches

3 medium-sized nectarines

3 medium-sized plums

1 cup blackberries

crème fraîche or Greek-style yoghurt, to serve

Preheat oven to 150°C.

Place butter, sugar, water and vanilla bean in a saucepan and stir gently until butter is just melted.

Cut peaches and nectarines in half and remove stones. Leave plums whole. Place fruit in ovenproof dish, cut-side up, in a single layer. Pour butter mixture over, place dish in preheated oven and bake for about 1 hour. Turn fruit occasionally and baste until fruit is soft and browned.

Serve warm or at room temperature with crème fraîche or yoghurt, drizzled with a little of the caramel sauce.

SERVES 6

Sour-cream, lime & passionfruit cake

125 g unsalted butter, softened

220 g caster sugar

1 teaspoon finely grated
lime zest

3 eggs, separated

300 g self-raising flour, sifted

1 cup sour cream mixed with
3 tablespoons freshly squeezed
lime juice

PASSIONFRUIT SYRUP

110 g caster sugar

strip of lime zest

½ cup water

pulp of 2 passionfruit

Preheat oven to 150°C. Grease a 24-cm springform cake pan and line with baking paper.

Beat butter, sugar and lime zest with an electric mixer until light and creamy. Add egg yolks one at a time, beating after each addition. Fold in half the flour and half the sour cream, mix well, then add the remainder and beat by hand until just combined.

Beat egg whites until soft peaks form, then fold lightly into batter in two batches, until well mixed. Pour cake mix into the prepared pan, place in preheated oven and bake for 1¼ hours. To test if cake is ready, insert a skewer into the centre – if it comes out clean, the cake is cooked. Leave in pan for a few minutes, then invert onto a cake rack to cool. **>**

To make passionfruit syrup, place sugar, lime zest and water in small saucepan, bring to the boil, stirring until sugar dissolves. Stir in passionfruit pulp and simmer for 6–8 minutes, using a spoon to skim any scum from surface. Remove lime zest and pour syrup over cooled cake.

SERVES 8

Tuscan apple & lemon cake

200 g plain flour
1 teaspoon baking powder
⅔ cup caster sugar
3 eggs
3 tablespoons unsalted butter, melted

⅓ cup milk
grated zest of 1 lemon
pinch of freshly grated nutmeg
3 golden delicious apples

Preheat oven to 180°C. Grease a 23-cm springform cake pan and line with baking paper.

Sift flour and baking powder into a medium-sized bowl. Add sugar, eggs, butter, milk, lemon zest and nutmeg, and beat with an electric beater until thick and smooth. Pour batter into prepared pan.

Peel, core and slice apples, and arrange in a circular pattern on top of batter. Place cake in preheated oven and bake for 1 hour. Check after about 50 minutes: if apples are beginning to burn, cover with baking paper or aluminium foil for the last 10 minutes. Cake is cooked when a skewer inserted in the centre comes out clean.

Remove cake from oven and let it cool slightly before removing from pan. Dust lightly with icing sugar and serve warm or at room temperature.

SERVES 6–8

Conversions

LIQUIDS

Millilitres	Fluid ounces
60 ml	2 fl oz
125 ml	4 fl oz
200 ml	6 fl oz
250 ml	8 fl oz
500 ml	16 fl oz
625 ml	20 fl oz (1 pint)

WEIGHTS

Grams	Ounces
30 g	1 oz
60 g	2 oz
90 g	3 oz
125 g	4 oz
250 g	8 oz
375 g	12 oz
500 g	16 oz (1 lb)
1 kg	2 lb

OVEN TEMPERATURES

Celsius	Fahrenheit
160°C	320°F
170°C	340°F
180°C	360°F
200°C	390°F
220°C	430°F

Index

Afghani Lamb with Chickpeas,
    Mint & Yoghurt 92
apples
    Pork Belly with Sage, Pancetta
        & Apples 144
    Red Cabbage Braised with Apple
        & Balsamic 212
    Tuscan Apple & Lemon Cake 248
apricots
    Beef with Apricots 96
Avocado Salsa 108

Baked Lime Delicious Pudding 224
Basque Chicken 56
beans, dried
    Cassoulet 106
    Chilli con Carne with Avocado Salsa
        & Sour Cream 108
    cooking 9
    La Ribollita 29
    Lamb & Lima-bean Soup with
        Fetta Toasts 31
    Lamb Shanks with Tomato, White Wine
        & White-bean Mash 133
    Lima Beans with Rosemary & Tomato 200
    Spicy Italian Sausages with Cannellini
        Beans 163
beef
    Beef with Apricots 96
    Beef Rendang 94
    Beef Stock 14
    Boeuf Bourguignon 98
    Bolognese Ragu 101
    Carbonnade of Beef 103

Chilli con carne with Avocado Salsa
    & Sour Cream 108
Classic Beef Goulash 111
cuts 4
Daube of Beef with Black-olive
    Tapenade 113
Family Beef & Vegetable Casserole 115
Oxtail Braise Moroccan-style 139
Oxtail Stew 142
Pot au Feu 150
Red Capsicums Stuffed with Beef
    & Pine Nuts 153
Spezzatino di Manzo 162
Steak & Kidney Pie 171
Steak & Mushroom Pie 173
beer
    Carbonnade of Beef 103
    Guinness Veal with Chat Potatoes 119
beetroot
    Oven-baked Beetroot with Yoghurt 205
    Russian Borscht 34
Boeuf Bourguignon 98
bok choy
    Slow-cooked Chinese Pork Belly
        with Bok Choy 161
Bolognese Ragu 101
Bouquet Garni 25
braising 3, 4–5
Braised Fennel 190
Brandade of Salt Cod 42

cakes
    Chocolate Cake with Chocolate
        Ganache 225

Golden Polenta & Olive Oil Cake 230
Scottish Dundee Cake 242
Sour-cream, Lime & Passionfruit Cake 245
Tuscan Apple & Lemon Cake 248
capsicums
    Red Capsicums Stuffed with Beef
        & Pine Nuts 153
Caramelised Baked Onions 191
Carbonnade of Beef 103
Cassoulet 106
Chermoula 47
cherries
    Dark Cherry Sauce 86
chicken
    Basque Chicken 56
    Chicken Baked in Thai Green Curry 58
    Chicken Chasseur, Slow-simmered 60
    Chicken, Mushroom & Thyme Braise 64
    Chicken Noodle Soup 16
    Chicken Stock 15
    Chicken Tagine 63
    Coq au Vin 66
    cuts 5, 55
    Jerez Chicken with Orange 77
    Persian Chicken with Walnuts
        & Pomegranate 80
    Saffron & Fennel Chicken 85
    Tuscan Sage Chicken with Soft Polenta 89
chickpeas
    Afghani Lamb with Chickpeas, Mint
        & Yoghurt 92
    canned 9–10
    Chickpea & Pancetta Soup 19
    Harira Soup 26
    Tagine of Lamb & Quince 175
Chilli con Carne with Avocado Salsa
    & Sour Cream 108
Chocolate Cake with Chocolate Ganache 225
Chocolate Jaffa Self-saucing Pudding 228

chutney
    Spiced Peach Chutney 147
Classic Beef Goulash 111
Classic Pea & Ham Soup 22
conversions 251
Coq au Vin 66
Couscous 192
    Herbed Couscous 192
    Nut and Berry Couscous 192
Creamy Mash 194
    Fetta Mash 194
    Horseradish Mash 194
    Mustard Mash 194
crockpots 10–11
Crumb Crust 106
curry
    Beef Rendang 94
    Chicken Baked in Thai Green Curry 58
custard
    Jane's Baked Nutmeg Custard 232

Dalmatian Fish Stew 44
Dark Cherry Sauce 86
Daube of Beef with Black-olive Tapenade 113
duck
    Cassoulet 106
    cuts 5, 55
    Duck Braised with Pink Peppercorns 68
    Duck Ragu with Pappardelle 71
    Slow-roasted Duck with Dark Cherry
        Sauce 86

eggplant
    Middle Eastern Eggplant & Lentil Stew 201

Family Beef & Vegetable Casserole 115
Farmer's Dijon Rabbit 74
fennel
    Braised Fennel 190

Saffron & Fennel Chicken 85
Tuscan Veal with Fennel 181
Fetta Mash 194
Fetta Toasts 31
fish *see* seafood
Florentine Roast Pork 116
French Onion Soup 23
fruit
Slow-roasted Summer Fruits with
Crème Fraîche 244
see also particular fruits

Golden Polenta & Olive Oil Cake 230
goulash
Classic Beef Goulash 111
Gremolata 195
Guinness Veal with Chat Potatoes 119

ham
Classic Pea & Ham Soup 22
Sunday-night Lentil & Ham Soup 38
Harira Soup 26
Herbed Couscous 192
Horseradish Mash 194

Indian Spice-crusted Leg of Lamb 122
Italian Lamb Ragu 125

Jane's Baked Nutmeg Custard 232
Jerez Chicken with Orange 77

kidneys
Steak & Kidney Pie 171

lamb
Afghani Lamb with Chickpeas, Mint &
Yoghurt 92
cuts 5
Harira Soup 26

Indian Spice-crusted Leg of Lamb 122
Italian Lamb Ragu 125
Lamb Hot Pot 127
Lamb & Lima-bean Soup with Fetta
Toasts 31
Lamb Shanks in an Oriental Braise 130
Lamb Shanks with Tomato, White Wine
& White-bean Mash 133
Rogan Josh 156
Scotch Broth 37
Shoulder of Lamb with Lemon & Saffron
158
Spicy Lamb and Red Lentils 166
Spring Navarin of Lamb 168
Tagine of Lamb & Quince 175
Traditional Shepherd's Pie 178
Leeks Braised in Red Wine 197
lemons
Gremolata 195
Lemon & Coriander Pilaf 198
Preserved Lemons 211
Shoulder of Lamb with Lemon
& Saffron 158
Tuscan Apple & Lemon Cake 248
lentils
cooking 9
Harira Soup 26
Middle Eastern Eggplant & Lentil Stew 201
Mujadarra (Lentils and Rice) 204
Spicy Lamb and Red Lentils 166
Sunday-night Lentil & Ham Soup 38
Tuscan Lentil Soup 39
Lima Beans with Rosemary & Tomato 200
limes
Baked Lime Delicious Pudding 224
Sour-cream, Lime & Passionfruit Cake 245

Middle Eastern Eggplant & Lentil Stew 201
Moroccan Fish Tagine with Chermoula 47

Mujadarra (Lentils and Rice) 204
mushrooms
    Chicken, Mushroom & Thyme Braise 64
    Steak & Mushroom Pie 173
Mustard Mash 194

noodles
    Chicken Noodle Soup 16
nuts
    Nut and Berry Couscous 192
    Pecan & Cranberry Bread-and-butter
        Pudding 237
    Persian Chicken with Walnuts
        & Pomegranate 80

Octopus Braised with Tomatoes
    & Red Wine 49
Old-fashioned Golden-syrup Pudding 233
olives
    Daube of Beef with Black-olive
        Tapenade 113
    Veal with Olives & Fetta Mash 185
onions
    Caramelised Baked Onions 191
    French Onion Soup 23
oranges
    Chocolate Jaffa Self-saucing Pudding 228
    Jerez Chicken with Orange 77
Osso Buco with Gremolata 136
Oven-baked Beetroot with Yoghurt 205
Oven-roasted Quinces with Star Anise 236
Oxtail Braise Moroccan-style 139
Oxtail Stew 142

pancetta
    Cassoulet 106
    Chickpea & Pancetta Soup 19
    Pork Belly with Sage, Pancetta
        & Apples 144

Rabbit with Pancetta & Basil 82
passionfruit
    Sour-cream, Lime & Passionfruit Cake 245
pasta
    Duck Ragu with Pappardelle 71
peaches
    Spiced Peach Chutney 147
pears
    Roasted Pears with Mascarpone 240
peas, dried
    Classic Pea & Ham Soup 22
Pecan & Cranberry Bread-and-butter Pudding
    237
Persian Chicken with Walnuts
    & Pomegranate 80
pies
    Steak & Kidney Pie 171
    Steak & Mushroom Pie 173
    Traditional Shepherd's Pie 178
pilaf
    Lemon & Coriander Pilaf 198
polenta
    Char-grilled Polenta 206
    Golden Polenta & Olive Oil Cake 230
    Soft Polenta 208
pomegranate
    Persian Chicken with Walnuts
        & Pomegranate 80
pork
    Cassoulet 106
    cuts 5
    Florentine Roast Pork 116
    Pork Belly with Sage, Pancetta
        & Apples 144
    Pork Roast & Spiced Peach Chutney 147
    Slow-cooked Chinese Pork Belly with
        Bok Choy 161
    Spicy Italian Sausages with Cannellini
        Beans 163

Pot au Feu 150
potatoes
    Brandade of Salt Cod 42
    Creamy Mash 194
    Fetta Mash 194
    Guinness Veal with Chat Potatoes 119
    Horseradish Mash 194
    Mustard Mash 194
    Potatoes Boulangère 209
    Rosemary Potatoes 217
    Skordalia 219
Preserved Lemons 211
puddings *see* sweets

quinces
    Oven-roasted Quinces with Star Anise 236
    Tagine of Lamb & Quince 175

rabbit
    cuts 5, 76
    Farmer's Dijon Rabbit 74
    Rabbit with Pancetta & Basil 82
ragu
    Bolognese Ragu 101
    Duck Ragu with Pappardelle 71
    Italian Lamb Ragu 125
Red Cabbage Braised with Apple
    & Balsamic 212
Red Capsicums Stuffed with Beef
    & Pine Nuts 153
Rendang Spice Paste 94
rice
    Lemon & Coriander Pilaf 198
    Mujadarra (Lentils and Rice) 204
    Risotto Milanese 214
Roasted Pears with Mascarpone 240
Rogan Josh 156
Rosemary Potatoes 217
Russian Borscht 34

saffron
    Saffron & Fennel Chicken 85
    Shoulder of Lamb with Lemon
        & Saffron 158
salsa
    Avocado Salsa 108
Salsa Verde 218
Salt-baked Ocean Trout 52
sausages
    Cassoulet 106
    Spicy Italian Sausages with Cannellini
        Beans 163
Scotch Broth 37
Scottish Dundee Cake 242
seafood
    Brandade of Salt Cod 42
    Dalmatian Fish Stew 44
    Moroccan Fish Tagine with Chermoula 47
    Octopus Braised with Tomatoes & Red
        Wine 49
    Salt-baked Ocean Trout 52
Shoulder of Lamb with Lemon
    & Saffron 158
Skordalia 219
slow-cookers 10–11
slow-cooking
    dairy products 11
    meat cuts 4–6
    pulses 9–10
    tips 6
Slow-cooked Chinese Pork Belly with Bok
    Choy 161
Slow-roasted Balsamic Tomatoes 220
Slow-roasted Duck with Dark Cherry
    Sauce 86
Slow-roasted Summer Fruits with Crème
    Fraîche 244
soups
    Chicken Noodle Soup 16

Chickpea & Pancetta Soup 19
Classic Pea & Ham Soup 22
French Onion Soup 23
Harira Soup 26
La Ribollita 29
Lamb & Lima-bean Soup with Fetta
    Toasts 31
Russian Borscht 34
Scotch Broth 37
Sunday-night Lentil & Ham Soup 38
Tuscan Lentil Soup 39
see also stocks
Sour-cream, Lime & Passionfruit Cake 245
Spezzatino di Manzo 162
Spiced Peach Chutney 147
Spicy Italian Sausages with Cannellini
    Beans 163
Spicy Lamb and Red Lentils 166
Spring Navarin of Lamb 168
Steak & Kidney Pie 171
Steak & Mushroom Pie 173
stewing 3, 4–5
stocks
    Beef Stock 14
    Chicken Stock 15
stove-top cooking 3–4
Sunday-night Lentil & Ham Soup 38
sweets
    Baked Lime Delicious Pudding 224
    Chocolate Jaffa Self-saucing Pudding 228
    Jane's Baked Nutmeg Custard 232
    Old-fashioned Golden-syrup Pudding 233
    Oven-roasted Quinces with Star Anise 236
    Pecan & Cranberry Bread-and-butter
        Pudding 237
    Roasted Pears with Mascarpone 240
    Slow-roasted Summer Fruits with Crème
        Fraîche 244
    see also cakes

tagine
    Chicken Tagine 63
    Moroccan Fish Tagine with Chermoula 47
    Tagine of Lamb & Quince 175
tomatoes
    Cassoulet 106
    Harira Soup 26
    Lamb Shanks with Tomato, White Wine &
        White-bean Mash 133
    Lima Beans with Rosemary & Tomato 200
    Octopus Braised with Tomatoes & Red
        Wine 49
    Slow-roasted Balsamic Tomatoes 220
    Tomato Passata 73
Traditional Shepherd's Pie 178
Tuscan Apple & Lemon Cake 248
Tuscan Lentil Soup 39
Tuscan Sage Chicken with Soft Polenta 89
Tuscan Veal with Fennel 181

veal
    cuts 5
    Guinness Veal with Chat Potatoes 119
    Osso Buco with Gremolata 136
    Tuscan Veal with Fennel 181
    Veal Chops Braised in White Wine 183
    Veal with Olives & Fetta Mash 185
vegetables
    Family Beef & Vegetable Casserole 115
    see also particular vegetables

wine
    Boeuf Bourguignon 98
    Bolognese Ragu 101
    Chicken Chasseur, Slow-simmered 60
    Coq au Vin 66
    Dark Cherry Sauce 86
    Duck Ragu with Pappardelle 71

Farmer's Dijon Rabbit 74
Italian Lamb Ragu 125
Lamb Shanks with Tomato, White Wine
    & White-bean Mash 133
Leeks Braised in Red Wine 197
Octopus Braised with Tomatoes & Red
    Wine 49

Oxtail Braise Moroccan-style 139
Spezzatino di Manzo 162
Veal Chops Braised in White Wine 183

yoghurt
    Oven-baked Beetroot with Yoghurt 205
    Yoghurt Sauce 92

PENGUIN BOOKS

Published by the Penguin Group
Penguin Group (Australia)
250 Camberwell Road, Camberwell, Victoria 3124, Australia
(a division of Pearson Australia Group Pty Ltd)

New York   Toronto   London   Dublin   New Delhi   Auckland   Johannesburg

Penguin Books Ltd, Registered Offices: 80 Strand, London, WC2R 0RL, England

First published by Penguin Group (Australia), 2008

10 9 8 7 6 5 4 3

Written by Margaret Barca
Text and photographs copyright © Penguin Group Australia, 2008

Cover and text design by Claire Tice © Penguin Group (Australia), 2008
Photography by Julie Renouf
Photography assistant Paul Nelson
Food styling by Linda Brushfield
Typeset in Mrs Eaves and Akzidenz Grotesk by Sunset Digital Pty Ltd
Scanning and separations by Splitting Image P/L, Clayton Victoria
Printed in China by Everbest Printing Co. Ltd

Many thanks to Creative Homewares in Albert Park, Market Imports and Matchbox in Armadale,
and Step Back Antiques in Hawthorn, for their lovely props.

Cataloguing information for this book is available
from the National Library of Australia

ISBN 978 014 300807 1

penguin.com.au

Muffin
BIBLE

Cake
BIBLE

Biscuit & Slice
BIBLE

Dessert
BIBLE

Noodle
BIBLE

Vegetarian
BIBLE

Salad
BIBLE

Seafood
BIBLE

Soup
BIBLE

Curry
BIBLE

Barbecue
BIBLE

cocktail
bible

party food
bible

Lunchbox
BIBLE

Also in this series

Food that satisfies the soul

Slow food doesn't mean taking forever to cook
a meal. It's about taking the time to enjoy good
food — choosing seasonal ingredients and
sharing the results with family and friends.

Most of the recipes in *Slow Food Bible* are simple
to prepare, and much of the time involved is
allowing the ingredients to simmer away while
you get on with other things, or simply kick
back and relax. There's a feast of recipes for
all seasons, from hearty braises to lighter
vegetables and sides and, of course, irresistible
year-round desserts. There are tips on using
slow-cookers, and for shortcuts that won't
compromise flavour and goodness.

Food / Cooking

ISBN 978-0-14-300807-1

9 780143 008071

penguin.com.au